D0699328

20.1.71

36.90

Casual Groups of Monkeys and Men

Stochastic Models of Elemental Social Systems

WITHDRAWN
UTSA LIBRARIES

Rapport entre la figure humaine et celle du singe.

[Figures 33A, 33B from] Dissertation sur un Traité de Charles le Brun [1619–1690], concernant le rapport de la Physionomie Humaine avec celle des Animaux; Ouvrage enrichi de la gravure des dessins tracés pour la demonstration de ce système. Paris, à la chalcographie du Musée Napoléon . . . 1806. [Chalcographie du Musée du Louvre, Paris]

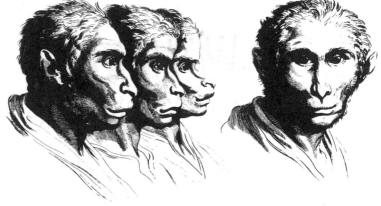

Casual Groups of Monkeys and Men

Joel E. Cohen

Stochastic Models of Elemental Social Systems

Harvard University Press
Cambridge, Massachusetts
1971

© Copyright 1971 by the RAND Corporation
All rights reserved
Distributed in Great Britain by Oxford University Press, London
Library of Congress Catalog Number: 73–133215
SBN 674–09981–8
Printed in the United States of America

Preface

The summer after I graduated from high school, I got a job at the University of Michigan running a psychological experiment that depended on a very complicated electronic apparatus. For seven of the ten weeks of my employment, the machine did not work. The beneficial consequences were two. First, in seven weeks of unrestricted reading in the university libraries, I found the article (Coleman and James 1961) in the then current issue of *Sociometry* which eventually led to this book. (Naturally, I may be the only one who considers this consequence beneficial.) Hours of observation in the basement cafeteria of the Michigan Union gave me distributions of group size not described by the Coleman model and convinced me that more remained to be done. Second, I learned to avoid complicated instrumentation in studying behavior if simpler tools would do. A stopwatch and pencil instrumented the empirical part of this study.

In 1963 Harrison C. White began moving minds, mine included, at Harvard. He raised then, and in my graduate years fulfilled, the prospect of expert stimulation and guidance in studying the questions his work (1962) posed. In the same year Edward O. Wilson introduced me to the evolutionary framework that motivates and makes sense out of this study's comparative approach. Irven B. DeVore made monkeys alluring enough in 1965 that I took primate studies seriously as a possible source of comparative data. And though I originally went to C. Frederick Mosteller for help in evaluating the data I already had, which were gathered by others, it was he who insisted that I make the observations of a new kind, on the dynamics of a system of social groups, which belong to the core of this book. In this whole undertaking, as in others before and since, Anthony G. Oettinger provided the umbrella of freedom, supported by the pillar of constructive criticism, which made the work possible. To these my teachers I am grateful for liberality of judgment about what is the proper sphere of science, together with high and conservative standards of what is good science.

Since completing this manuscript over a year ago, I have enjoyed the support and hospitality of Stuart and Jeanne Altmann during two months of observing baboon social behavior. Observations made in Kenya in 1969 confirm that the equilibrium size distributions of freely forming baboon social groups are consistent with the predictions of the LOST models presented here. A brief report will appear in the *Proceedings of the Third International Congress of Primatology* (Zurich 1970). In addition, I have learned of work by J. F. C. Kingman [*Journal of Applied Probability* (1969), 1–18] on models he calls Markov population processes. The tools he presents may answer some of the analytical problems encountered here and may make possible the analysis of new sociological models.

For reading, criticising, and immeasurably improving previous drafts of this work, I am grateful to Stuart A. Altmann, William H. Bossert, Robert H. MacArthur, C. Frederick Mosteller, Anthony G. Oettinger, Ganapati P. Patil, and Harrison C. White. For the use of previously unpublished data or for access to private records from which I compiled data, I thank Paul A. Berger, Frank A. Haight, P. A. Morris, Robert Novak, and Thomas T. Struhsaker. Stuart A. Altmann directed me to the data in Struhsaker's thesis. Doris Siever opened the playrooms of Cambridge Nursery School to me. Donald G. M. Anderson, Richard H. Bolt, William G. Cochran, Milton Kamins, Leo Katz, Carl N. Morris, and Carol D. Watson helped on varied technical points. Through Edward S. Quade, The RAND Corporation patiently saw the manuscript to its final form. The Milton Fund of Harvard University supported computational and other expenses.

In the beginning, as in the end, is Harvard's Society of Fellows. I believe it to be no accident that my boss in the summer of 1961, James G. Miller, who let me entertain myself when I was not needed for work, is a former Junior Fellow of the Society. A decade later in my final year as a Junior Fellow, the Society remains a cornucopia of freedom

and resources perfused with the expectation of good work
and the company of energetic talent.

These pages are dedicated to Audrey, who forms with me
a group that is beyond the scope of this book.

J.E.C.

Adams House
14 June 1970

Contents

Tables

Figures

Casual Groups of Monkeys and Men

Stochastic Models of Elemental Social Systems

Sociology is the science which has the most methods and the fewest results. Therefore it is by the regular facts that it is proper to begin.
Henri Poincaré,
The Value of Science

Any one will renovate his science who will steadily look after the irregular phenomena.
William James,
The Powers and Limitations of Science

1.1 Overview

Who sleeps with whom interests primates of several species. A wild East African vervet monkey (*Cercopithecus aethiops*) has a participant's lively interest in the formation of sleeping groups within his troop every evening. To a human observer of a vervet troop, the formation of these sleeping groups offers an opportunity to improve his understanding of social behavior and organization from an evolutionary perspective. Study of an animal's society also offers a human observer a middle ground between studies of individual behavior and of population ecology; and it may provide a link between them.

Previous studies of freely forming small groups of humans showed that the observed frequency distributions of the number of individuals in a group were usually very closely described by the Poisson distribution with the zero value truncated (Section 1.2). Several models, based on widely varying assumptions, were proposed to account for the observed regularity. The multiplicity of these models posed the challenge of finding data that would discriminate among them. Nonhuman primate data with the detail necessary to make discriminations offered the further possible

3

advantage of requiring a model of some evolutionary generality.

During a year's field study of wild vervet monkeys in East Africa, Thomas T. Struhsaker recorded individual by individual the composition of the sleeping groups of a particular troop on 22 nights (Section 1.3). On an additional 16 nights he was able to observe the composition or size of some, but not all, of the sleeping groups of the troop. The frequency distribution of the sizes of these groups cannot be described by a truncated Poisson distribution, so the models constructed for human groups cannot apply directly to the monkeys.

But the frequency distribution of the sizes of the monkey groups is well described by a negative binomial distribution with the zero value truncated (Section 2.1). A truncated negative binomial distribution can arise as a compound truncated Poisson distribution. Finer analysis of the data shows, however, that the distribution of group sizes is not a time-varying truncated Poisson (Section 2.2); nor is it compounded of truncated Poisson processes associated with each individual, the parameters of which vary from one monkey to another (Section 2.3). Thus plausible attempts to reduce the formation of groups to a mixture of humanlike truncated Poisson processes fail.

A combinatorial model that counts the number of arrangements of distinguishable individuals in indistinguishable groups and assumes all such arrangements equiprobable fails to approximate the observed distribution of number of groups per night (Section 3.1). Another combinatorial model succeeds in approximating both the distribution of number of groups per night and the distribution of group sizes, with the help of an ad hoc assumption that no more groups may exist than were observed on the night with the highest number of groups (Section 3.2). This model counts the number of arrangements of indistinguishable individuals in indistinguishable groups. But the model must be rejected because it assumes the monkeys to be indistinguishable and because it predicts only monotonic decreasing frequency density functions.

A family of simple stochastic models, formally like some of the models previously proposed for the human data, involves rates of joining and leaving groups that are linear functions of group size (Chapter 4). The number of isolates (groups of size 1) in the system is assumed to affect directly only the formation of pairs and then to have no direct effect on the formation of larger groups.

To be interpretable, these models, called the linear one-step transition (LOST) models, can have only two independent parameters. The models assume that individuals join groups because of the attraction of either group membership or individuals in the group, and that they leave groups for independent, individual reasons. The first parameter describes the ratio of the rate of joining because of the attraction of group membership to the rate of leaving. The second parameter describes the ratio of the rate of joining because of the attraction of individuals in groups to the rate of leaving. In the interpretable ranges of these parameters, the models predict at equilibrium a distribution of group sizes given by the truncated negative binomial distribution. A special value of one of the parameters leads to the truncated Poisson distribution.

The behavior of isolates can be so specified that the LOST models describe either a system of groups with a fixed number of individuals (defined as a "closed" system, whether or not the number of groups varies), or a system with a variable number of individuals (defined as an "open" system) in which the number of groups is constant. In either case, the form of the equilibrium size distribution remains the same.

Numerical solution of the system of ordinary differential equations, deterministically interpreted, that define the open and closed models gives information about how average systems of groups move toward equilibrium from various initial conditions (Section 4.4). When the rate constants of the model are estimated from the flux of individuals among groups (Section 5.4), that information about the rapidity of approach to equilibrium makes possible a decision about whether a particular system of groups is near equilibrium.

The free play of four-year-olds at the Cambridge Nursery School was observed to test the detailed mechanisms of group formation assumed by the LOST models (Section

5.1). The number of groups of each size in the playroom was recorded at 30-second intervals (data are in Section 5.1). The frequency distributions of group size, cumulated for each day of observation, are consistent with the equilibrium predicted by the LOST models (Section 5.3).

Comparison of the numbers of groups of each size at each epoch of observation with the numbers in the following epoch gives estimates of the parameters of arrival and departure (Section 5.4). According to a technique of measuring variability called the "jackknife" (Appendix A to Chapter 5), these estimates of the parameters of the model, called the "dynamic" estimates, did not differ significantly from the estimates of the corresponding parameters obtained from the equilibrium distribution, when the children were playing freely without adult intervention.

Though the parameters estimated from the nursery school observations varied from day to day, a stochastic simulation of an open LOST process (Appendix B to Chapter 5) shows that the observed variability in parameter estimates is no greater than could be attributed to small-sample fluctuations from an underlying process with constant parameters. Thus, the rates of arrival and departure could be assumed to have been constant during the weeks in which observations were made.

The detailed data and analysis in Chapter 5 suggest that the dynamics of the linear one-step transition models proposed in Chapter 4 approximate the real process by which casual social groups form and dissolve over a period of time —at least in the free play of four-year-old humans.

Those linear stochastic models account not only for the size distribution of Struhsaker's monkey groups and the dynamics and equilibrium of nursery school play; they also account for two of the three distributions of the sizes of pedestrian human groups that had previously resisted interpretation (Section 6.1) and for at least two of the (possibly biased) distributions of the sizes of sleeping groups of four other species of monkeys observed in Uganda (Section 6.2). The linear models may account for the distribution of the occupancy of passenger cars on Los Angeles freeways as well (Section 6.3), though further details are needed.

In several instances, including the formation of international alliances for war, the LOST models fail to predict observed distributions when the assumptions underlying the predictions are clearly violated (Section 6.4). Thus the LOST models offer some possibility of understanding why good predictions are obtained when they are.

Struhsaker's social data reveal interesting individual differences among the monkeys (Section 7.1). Whereas the relative frequency of isolates among groups is, as expected, binomially distributed when the identity of the monkeys is ignored, the relative frequency of isolation for each monkey departs strikingly from the binomial distribution that might be expected. Obvious factors such as age, sex, and social rank do not in most cases explain why some monkeys slept alone much more often than was expected, and why others never did.

The formation of sleeping groups seems to be one facet of the troop's social life where dominance is not important (Section 7.2), according to Struhsaker's data. The diverse social composition of these groups renders less plausible one role proposed for the sleeping groups by Struhsaker: the gradual formation of new, independent troops.

Given the form of the distribution of group sizes, the parameters of the distribution can be fairly well calculated, at least in the case of human groups, from an acoustical theory that links individual requirements and capacities for understanding speech with ecological information about background noise levels (Section 7.3). That derivation exemplifies how explicit theory can unify independent measurements of individual organisms, social organization, and the environment.

The variety of data, models, and questions about the relations between models and data that have been mentioned briefly here will be presented more fully in the following chapters. Since there is not always a one-to-one correspondence between the questions posed by the various models and the answers provided by the different kinds of data, the path is somewhat complicated. Section 3.3 provides a roadside progress report. At the end of the journey, Section 8.1 provides a map in the form of a matrix summarizing the relation between each model or distribution and each set of data. Reference to those two sections, and to this section, should allay confusion about the more detailed parts of the exposition.

The final chapter attempts to evaluate critically the claims and accomplishments of the whole work and to raise questions that could be resolved by future experiments, observational studies, and theories. The conclusion argues that explicit models of social organization backed by sufficient data can contribute to clearer language and more useful concepts for comparative and evolutionary discussions of human and nonhuman societies.

1.2 Size Distribution of Spontaneous Human Groups

James (1951, 1953) recorded the size of 15,486 freely forming small groups in 18 different situations. The resulting frequency distributions of group size, plus another 2,509 observations in three other situations, are published in full in Coleman (1964:368–373). James (1951:475) defined these small groups as

groups in which the members were in face-to-face interaction as evidenced by the criteria of gesticulation, laughter, smiles, talk, play or work. Individuals who merely occupied contiguous space were not counted as members of a group. Finally, all observations were carried out by teams of two, namely, a counter and a recorder.

James (1953:569) defined "free-forming" groups as

those whose members are relatively free to maintain or break off contact with one another, that is, they are ones where informal controls on behavior are at work and spontaneity is at a maximum.

James observed situations such as pedestrians in Eugene, Oregon, on a spring morning; shopping groups in two Portland, Oregon, department stores; play groups in the spring on the playgrounds of 14 elementary schools in Eugene (directed or organized play was not included in the observations); public gatherings at a public beach swimming pool in Portland in the spring; and pedestrians moving past a designated sidewalk spot in Seoul, Korea.

Coleman and James (1961; see also Coleman 1964:361–368) observed that nearly all of the frequency distributions of the sizes of those groups were very closely described by the Poisson distribution with the zero value truncated. Coleman proposed a model for the frequency distribution of sizes of a single group, based on that group's probabilities of transition from one size to another. That model predicts at equilibrium a truncated Poisson distribution of group size. Coleman took the fit of the observed distributions of size in collections of groups as confirmation of the model.

White (1962:156) pointed out that "the state of a system [of groups] must be specified by the number of groups of each size" and that the step from a model pertaining to a single group to a model pertaining to a system of groups must be argued, if it is valid at all. White claimed to derive the truncated Poisson distribution as the equilibrium frequency distribution of group sizes from a variety of grossly different models pertaining to systems of groups. These models varied in

assumptions about recruitment [of individuals] from the environment, the channels through which circulation of members proceeds, and the dependence of rates of both joining and leaving groups on both the sizes and numbers of groups (White 1962:153).

Some of his models had fixed numbers of individuals (closed systems); in others, individuals could enter or leave the system (open systems). Some had fixed numbers of groups; in others the number of groups varied. Since a variety of models appears to lead to the same equilibrium distribution, White concluded that

more elaborate empirical investigations . . . will be needed to test the applicability of and to discriminate among simple stochastic models for the circulation of members among casual groups (1962:154).

Goodman (1964) concurred in this conclusion, although, after a detailed criticism of the Coleman-James model and one of White's models, he pointed out that these models lead to the truncated Poisson distribution only in very special cases not specified in the previous discussion. Goodman suggested applying to systems of groups an n-group emigration-immigration model (Section 2.3), which can lead to a zero-truncated Poisson distribution of group sizes or to a zero-truncated negative binomial distribution.

Thus, James discovered a striking regularity in the social aggregations of large collections of people, while Coleman, White, and Goodman provided several different explanations, each accompanied with a plea for further empirical research.

Prior to the work of all American students of group size and unknown to them was the work of two Japanese scientists, Hirata (1933) and Terao (1949). They showed "that the number of persons in a group may be (truncated) Poisson" (Haight 1967:105). (I have been unable to locate these articles.)

1.3 Struhsaker's Data on Vervet Monkeys

Field studies of the behavior of free-ranging primates have recently increased enormously in number, objectivity, and depth (DeVore 1965; Altmann 1967). Those studies often include observations of the organization of primate societies, sometimes with metaphorical comparative remarks on human social organization. One sociologist (Henshel 1963) proposed, but did not carry out, a systematic test of theories of human dominance with observations of nonhuman primates.

What follows here is an attempt at a systematic comparative study of one aspect—the distribution of sizes of casual groups—of primate social organization. Data on the formation of groups in nonhuman primate societies can show whether the regularity in James's data holds for more than one (the human) species; and if they are sufficiently detailed, the data may discriminate among available models. Interpretation of these data may also help to develop clearer language and concepts in discussions of the evolution of human and nonhuman societies.

A fourteen-month-long field study of wild East African

vervet monkeys by Thomas T. Struhsaker provided data of the detail and quality desired. Struhsaker (1967a) has given a general comparison of the results of his study with previous findings on other cercopithecine monkeys. More details on behavior and vocalizations appear in Struhsaker (1967b and 1967d).

Struhsaker describes the social behavior of interest to this study:

Nearly every evening, just before sunset (between 1830 and 1900 hours), the vervet groups [which we shall refer to as troops] divided into sleeping subgroups [which we shall refer to as groups] that spent the night separated from one another by at least one impassable break in the tree canopy. It is most certain that the vervets did not climb to the ground after sunset nor before sunrise and thus these subgroups [groups] were isolated from one another throughout the night . . . They reunited after sunrise, usually before 0800 hours . . . Between February 1964 and June 1964, the 1530 group was checked at sunset and the following sunrise for subgroup formation on 52 different occasions. Subgroups were formed 51 times and once the entire group slept together in a grove of trees united by a continuous tree canopy (1967c: 110).

In his Ph.D. dissertation, Struhsaker continues:

The most abundant and reliable data on sleeping subgroup composition were obtained from the 1530 group and are summarized in [the list that follows]. Only those nights on which all members of the group were accounted for are included in this [list](1965:132).

That criterion of selection would seem biased against nights in which the troop was excessively spread out in the tree tops. Hence, nights in which there were many small groups might be underrepresented. However, Struhsaker (personal communication, 17 June 1968) feels that the density of foliage in the sleeping trees was a more important possible source of bias than the dispersion of the troop. When the monkeys slept in trees with very dense foliage, they were less likely to be identified. If larger

11

groups of monkeys tended to use trees or groves with denser foliage, then nights in which there were large groups would be underrepresented in the data. Those two sources of bias oppose each other, but the size of the effect due to each is unknown.

Since Struhsaker's data are by far the best available for the present purposes, they will be used as they are. Previously unreported data of Struhsaker's (personal communication, 17 June 1968), which are summarized in Table 1.3 confirm that those sources of bias are probably negligible, as far as the major conclusions of this study are concerned.

Struhsaker's observations of the composition of sleeping groups in the 1530 troop of vervet monkeys follow (1965: 299–301). The age, sex, and some of the kinship characteristics of the individuals are also given. (Those characteristics we ignore until forced to reconsider them in Chapter 7.) Groups are separated by parentheses, and all notation is Struhsaker's.

I = adult male SG

II = the older adult male (left the troop between 17–18 April and 27–28 April 1964)

III = adult male LP

IV = adult female DK

V = juvenile male LYA

VI = adult female TK

VII = young juvenile female D

VIII = young juvenile female B

IX = young juvenile female DR

X = juvenile female NN

XI = subadult female N

XII = adult female TBW

XIII = two young indistinguishable juvenile males

XIV = infant male DK (son of IV)

XV = infant female TBW (born to XII between 4–5 Jan. and 29–30 Jan. 1964)

XVI = infant male TK (born to VI between 29–30 Jan. and 4–5 Feb. 1964)

Date	Groups	
4–5 Jan. 1964	(IV, XIV, XIII), (I, III, V, XII, XIII), (XI, IX, X), (II), (VIII, VII, VI)	Introduction
29–30 Jan. 1964	(VI, X, VIII, VII, IX), (I, II, III, IV, XIV, XII, XV, V, XI, XIII, XIII)	
4–5 Feb. 1964	(V, XIII, XIII, IV, XIV, II, XII, XV, XI), (I), (III), (VIII, IX, VII, X, VI, XVI)	
9–10 Feb. 1964	(III, II, V), (I, XI, XIII, XIII), (X, IX), (VIII, VII, VI, XVI, IV, XIV, XII, XV)	
23–24 Feb. 1964	(XII, XV, XI), (other 14)	
24–25 Feb. 1964	(I, III, XI), (other 14)	
1–2 March 1964	(XII, XV, XI, III), (other 13)	
9–10 March 1964	(X), (XI, III, XIII, XII, XV), (V, I, IX, VII, VIII, VI, XVI, IV, XIV, II, XIII)	
31 March 1964– 1 Apr. 1964	(III, XIII, X), (XI, IX), (II, XII, XV), (I, VII, VIII, V, IV, XIV, VI, XVI, XIII)	
1–2 April 1964	(II, XII, XV), (XI, XIII, IX), (IV, XIV, XIII), (VI, XVI, VII, VIII, III, I, V, X)	
4–5 April 1964	(I, II), (VI, XVI), (III, X), (V), (VII, VIII, IX, XII, XV, XIII, XIII, XI, IV, XIV)	
6–7 April 1964	(IV, XIV, XIII, XIII, XI, IX), (III, XII, XV, VI, XVI, VIII, X), (II, I, VII, V)	
17–18 April 1964	(X), (IV, XIV, XIII, XIII, IX, XI), (III, XII, XV), (I, V, VI, XVI, VII, VIII), (II)	
27–28 April 1964	(I, IX, V, X, XIII, III), (XII, XV), (XI), (IV, XIV, XIII, VIII, VII, VI, XVI)	
30 April 1964– 1 May 1964	(IV, XIV, XIII, IX, X), (I, XI, XII, XV), (VI, XVI, VII, VIII, XIII, V), (III)	
4–5 May 1964	(VI, XVI), (IV, XIV, XIII), (III, XII, XV), (I, XI), (X, XIII, VII, VIII, IX), (V)	
9–10 May 1964	(XIII, IX, XI), (III, I, V, XIII), (XII, XV), (VI, XVI, VII, VIII), (IV, XIV), (X)	
11–12 May 1964	(XII, XV), (IX, III, XIII, X), (XI), (I, V, IV, XIV, XIII), (VI, XVI, VII, VIII)	13

19–20 May 1964	(XI, IX, I), (III), (V, XII, XV, VII, VIII, X, VI, XVI, XIII), (XIII, IV, XIV)
21–22 May 1964	(VI, XVI, VII, VIII), (III), (XI, IX), (XII, XV), (I), (IV, XIV, XIII, XIII, X, V)
1–2 June 1964	(XII, XV), (XI), (XIII, V, X, IV, XIV, IX, I), (XIII, VI, XVI, VII, VIII), (III)
4–5 June 1964	(XII, XV, V), (XI), (XIII, IV, XIV), (I, X, IX, XIII), (VI, XVI, VII, VIII), (III)

In the course of these observations two births occurred and one individual (II) left the troop. Still, the rate of change in the composition of the whole troop was so much less than the rate of change of composition of sleeping groups from night to night that we will view the data as observations on a closed system, one with no immigration or emigration. (In Section 4.3 we will consider a model that does not require the system to be closed.)

On 16 nights, in addition to the one night in which the whole troop slept in one group and the 22 nights recorded above, Struhsaker was able to observe some, but not all, of the monkeys in the 1530 troop. On those 16 nights he determined exactly the number of animals in 55 sleeping groups. He kindly made those previously unpublished data available to me (personal communication, 17 June 1968). I exclude from the data one group on which he commented "possibly others present here."

The available data may be summarized as follows: ($G = G' + G''$ is an unknown number of groups to be estimated.)

					Total
Number of nights	1	22	16	13	(52)
Number of groups	1	91	$55 + G'$	G''	$(147 + G)$

The only available information about the remaining 13 nights is that the monkeys formed into two or more sleeping groups.

We use this information to estimate two distributions: the number of groups per night, and the size of groups. To estimate the first, we will assume that each night is an independent random sample from the population of nights; to estimate the second, we will assume that each group size is an independent random sample from the population of group sizes.

These two assumptions are not necessarily mutually compatible, but they may be so according to certain models of how the monkeys form groups from night to night (such as the LOST models in Chapter 4). The use of either assumption in comparing either estimated distribution with the predictions of a particular model will have to be justified by the model.

To estimate the frequency distribution of the number of groups per night, assuming each night is an independent random observation, we note that on 1 out of the 52 nights, one sleeping group was observed; so the maximum likelihood estimate of the proportion of such nights is 1/52. Let G_j be the number of nights, out of the 22 listed above on which j groups were formed, $j = 2, 3, \ldots$. The values of G_j are listed in Table 1.1. If the distribution of the number

Table 1.1. Frequency Distribution of the Number of Vervet Sleeping Groups per Night

Number of groups	Frequency
2	4
3	2
4	7
5	5
6	4
Mean = 4.136 Variance = 1.838	N = 22

Data from Struhsaker (1965: 299-301).

of groups were the same during the 22 listed nights as during the rest of the period of observation, then the relative frequency $G_j/22$ of j groups would predict an absolute frequency $51G_j/22$ of j groups during the 51 out of 52 nights when more than one group was observed. Hence, there would be an overall relative frequency (probability) of j groups equal to $(51/52)G_j/22, j = 2, 3, \ldots$, and an over-all relative frequency (probability) of one group equal to 1/52. To compare this distribution with fitted distributions using the χ^2 test, it is convenient to convert these estimated probabilities to estimated absolute frequencies, which should reflect the actual number (23) of observations on which the probabilities are based. Multiplying the esti-mated probabilities by 23 gives the estimated frequency of one group per night in a sample of 23 nights as 23/52 and the estimated frequency of $j \geq 2$ groups per night in a sample of 23 nights as $(51/52)(23/22)G_j = 1.025G_j$. Round-ing these estimated frequencies to the nearest whole num-ber gives exactly the frequencies G_j listed in Table 1.1, which will be used henceforth.

To estimate the frequency distribution of group size, assuming each group size is an independent random ob-servation, we again assume that the distribution of the num-ber of groups was the same during the 22 listed nights as during the rest of the period of observation. Since 91 groups were observed during those 22 nights, under ideal condi-tions a total of $(91/22)52 = 215.09 \approx 215$ groups would have been observed during the 52 nights. Of these, one would have been of size 17 (the whole troop). Let S_j be the number of groups of size j found during the 22 listed nights, $j < 17$. Then, as before, the relative frequency (probability) of groups of size j would be estimated, based on the sample of 215 groups, to be $(214/215)S_j/91, j = 1,$ $2, \ldots, 16$. Again, to convert these estimated probabilities to estimated absolute frequencies based on the actual number of observations (91 plus 1), it is necessary to multiply through by 92. Then the estimated absolute frequency of groups of size 17 is 92/215 and of smaller size j is $(214/215)(92/91)S_j = 1.006S_j$. Rounding these estimated frequencies to the nearest whole number gives exactly the frequencies S_j listed in Table 1.2, which will be used henceforth.

But the frequencies in Table 1.2 do not take advantage of the additional 55 group sizes Struhsaker observed on nights when he could not observe the whole troop. Let Q_j be the absolute frequency of groups of size j among the $91 + 55 = 146$ groups observed, $j = 1, 2, \ldots, 16$. On the basis of these

Size of group	Observed frequency	Truncated Poisson	Truncated negative binomial
1	19	7.3	18.9
2	14	14.3	17.1
3	19	18.6	14.1
4	11	18.1	11.0
5	7	14.1	8.3
6	7	9.2	6.2
7	3	5.1	4.5
8	2	2.5	3.2
9	3	1.1	2.3
10	1	0.4	1.6
11	2	0.1	1.1
12	0	1.7 { 0.0	1.4 { 0.8
13	1	0.0	0.6
14	2	0.0	1.2 { 0.4
>14	0	0.0	0.8
Mean = 3.978	N = 91	$\lambda = 3.897$	$r = 1.744$
Variance = 9.222		$X^2 = 57.327$	$p = 0.341$
		df = 7	$X^2 = 5.228$
		$P < 0.001$	df = 10
			$0.8 < P < 0.9$

Data from Struhsaker (1965: 299-301).

observations, the relative frequency of groups of size j in a sample of 215 groups would have been $(214/215)Q_j/146$, while the relative frequency of groups of size 17 would have been, as usual, $1/215$. Then the estimated absolute frequency of groups of size j in a sample of $147 = 146 + 1$ observations would be $(214/215)(147/146)Q_j = 1.002Q_j$, $j = 1, 2, \ldots, 16$; the estimated absolute frequency of groups of size 17 would be $147/215$. Rounding these to the nearest whole number gives exactly the frequencies listed in Table 1.3: simply the union of the observations of the 22 listed nights, Struhsaker's unpublished 55 group sizes, and the one night when all the monkeys slept together. These frequencies will be used henceforth.

The remainder of this chapter shows that the observed frequency distributions of group sizes (Tables 1.2 and 1.3) in a vervet monkey troop are not adequately described by a

17

Table 1.3. Frequency Distribution of Size of Vervet Sleeping Groups[a]

Size of group	Observed frequency		Truncated negative binomial	
1	27		28.3	
2	29		26.8	
3	24		22.8	
4	20		18.2	
5	12		14.0	
6	9		10.5	
7	5		7.7	
8	4		5.6	
9	9		4.0	
10	2		2.8	
11	2		2.0	
12	0		1.4	
13	1	} 3	1.0	} 1.7
14	2		0.7	
15	0		0.5	
16	0	} 1	0.3	} 1.4
17	1		0.2	
>17			0.4	

$$p = 0.351$$
$$r = 1.920$$
$$x^2 = 11.599$$
$$df = 11$$
$$0.3 < P < 0.5$$

Data from Struhsaker (1965: 299-301 and personal communication 17 June 1968).
[a] Included are nights when some animals in the troop were not seen.

truncated Poisson distribution, equation (1.1) below. Hence, the models of social kinetics that lead to the truncated Poisson are not immediately applicable. A reader who is willing to accept this conclusion may wish to skip to the next chapter, which is devoted to seeing whether any of those models leading to the truncated Poisson can be salvaged by a finer analysis of the data. Such a reader should be warned that some of the tools and tests to be introduced in Section 1.4 will be used later in the book; however, it may be sufficient to check the details then.

1.4 Statistical Detour

Next to the observed distribution in Table 1.2 is a theoretical Poisson distribution truncated at zero

$$P(k|\lambda) = \frac{\lambda^k}{(e^\lambda - 1)k!}, \qquad k = 1, 2, 3, \ldots, \qquad (1.1)$$

which has been fitted to this distribution. The maximum-likelihood estimate of $\lambda = 3.8972$, based on the mean, was obtained by linear interpolation in the table of Cohen (1960:205). (A slightly less convenient alternative would have been the table in Barton, David, and Merrington, 1960.)

In order to test validly the fit of the observed distribution to the theoretical with the χ^2 test, the observations of group size must all be independent, as has been assumed. Since the same animals compose the troop from day to day, the groups are not physically independent from day to day; and Struhsaker (1967c) has shown that some individuals (mothers and their infants, for example) appear together in sleeping groups much more often than could be accounted for by random pairing. In spite of the nonindependence from night to night of the composition of sleeping groups, it will be assumed that the mixing of animals during the day, when the sleeping groups rejoin to form the troop, is sufficient to render the sizes of groups independent from night to night.

Since there are only 17 monkeys in the troop, if group sizes are independently drawn from a truncated (below 1) Poisson distribution, that distribution must also be truncated above 17. As an approximation, the truncation above 17 will be ignored, since the predicted frequency above 17 is very small, with the parameter value as estimated.

Not only is group composition not independent from night to night, and group size limited to 17, but the sizes of groups on a given night cannot be independent, since they must sum to 17 (or however many monkeys there are in the troop at the time). Thus, given all but one of the group sizes on a night, we can take their sum and subtract from 17 to find the remaining group size. This calculation is possible only for nights, like Struhsaker's 22, when all the animals were observed. For the 55 group sizes included in Table 1.3, such a calculation is impossible.

If groups of the same size from different nights are counted together, as in Table 1.2, in a frequency distribution having k cells, the constraint of fixed troop size and the knowledge of the number of nights of observation make it possible to predict the frequency of any one group size from a knowledge of all the other frequencies, because the number of nights times troop size equals the total numbers of individuals observed on all nights. However, this information is no more than simply knowledge of the total number of groups observed and of all but one of the frequencies of group sizes. Therefore, the constraint of fixed troop size does not reduce the degrees of freedom of the frequency distribution below the number, $k - 1$, left when the total frequency is known.

Since, in the frequency distribution of group size, it is not possible to predict the size of one group from knowledge of the number of groups of the same size, the χ^2 test * may be used to determine whether the observations of group size could have been drawn independently from a truncated Poisson distribution, without considering any model that might have yielded that distribution. The use of the χ^2 test of goodness of fit or of any others with "sociological" models (such as those of Chapter 4) in which group sizes interact must be explicitly justified (see Appendix to Chapter 4).

Under the assumptions of independence, we pool the frequencies of groups of sizes 9 through 14. The resulting X^2 value is much too large to have arisen by chance. (Cochran 1954 supports the use of the χ^2 test with theoretical cell frequencies as small as 1 in the tails of unimodel distributions like the Poisson and negative binomial.) Hence the assumption that the underlying distribution of group sizes is truncated Poisson may be rejected.

* Throughout, we maintain the distinction between χ^2, the distribution of the sum of squares of standardized normal variates, and X^2, an estimate or estimator of χ^2 under some null hypothesis. Neither of those is to be confused with the notation $\bar{x}$ for the sample mean. Here we follow the notation of Cochran (1954) and Kendall and Stuart (1958).

For later use, it is convenient to present here another
method that reveals a certain failure of the observed frequency distribution to fit a Poisson distribution truncated
at zero (Fisher 1958:57–63). In the nontruncated Poisson,
the theoretical mean equals the theoretical variance. It
can be shown that if s^2 is the unbiased estimate of the variance, and $\bar{x}$ is the sample mean, then asymptotically,

$$X^2 = \frac{(T-1)s^2}{\bar{x}} \qquad (1.2)$$

has the distribution of χ^2 with $T-1$ degrees of freedom,
where T equals the number of independent observations.
The expression (1.2), due to Fisher, measures whether the
observed distribution is over- or underdispersed, that is,
whether the variance is too large or too small. (The expression for this test given by Goodman 1964:190, Eq. (89) is
incorrect.)

In the truncated Poisson distribution (truncated at zero
henceforth), the mean $\mu' = \lambda/(1-e^{-\lambda})$ is related to the
variance $(\sigma')^2$ as follows:

$$(\sigma')^2 = \frac{\lambda}{1-e^{-\lambda}}\left[1 - \frac{\lambda e^{-\lambda}}{1-e^{-\lambda}}\right] = \mu'(1-p_1'), \qquad (1.3)$$

where $p_1' = \lambda/(e^{\lambda}-1)$ is the probability of groups of size
one. Hence (Rao and Chakravarti 1956), the expression

$$X^2 = \frac{(T-1)s^2}{(1-p_1')\bar{x}} \qquad (1.4)$$

asymptotically for large samples has the distribution of
χ^2 with $T-1$ degrees of freedom, where p_1' is calculated
with the estimate of λ obtained from Cohen (1960), and T
again is the number of independent observations. Expression (1.2) will be referred to as the Poisson variance test,
and (1.4) as the truncated Poisson variance test.

For Table 1.2, $\lambda = 3.8972$ as before, $T = 91$, and $X^2 =$
226.96 according to (1.4) with df = 90. Converting that value
of X^2 to a standardized normal variate gives $z = 8.00$. The

21

observed distribution is clearly too dispersed to be truncated Poisson.

Similarly for the distribution of Table 1.3: since the mean is $\bar{x} = 4.0748$, $\lambda = 3.995$, and $T = 147$, we get $X^2 = 367.20$ with df $= 146$. The corresponding value of a standardized normal variate is 10.04, so again the distribution is not truncated Poisson.

Since the degrees of freedom of the truncated variance test depend not on the number of cells in a frequency distribution but on the number of independent observations, it may be that the degrees of freedom assigned for Table 1.2 should be reduced by 22, and those for Table 1.3 by 23, the number of nights, respectively, when the group totals were fixed. In both cases, reducing the degrees of freedom only strengthens the conclusion that the observed distributions are not drawn from the truncated Poisson.

The test (1.4) really understates whatever overdispersion may be present if the null hypothesis is a Poisson distribution truncated below 1 and above 17, because the relation (1.3) between mean and variance ignores the effect of truncation above 17. That truncation makes the true variance even smaller with respect to the mean, hence the true denominator in (1.4) ought to be smaller than it is and X^2 should be larger. Thus, whenever we reject the truncated Poisson by this test (1.4), we err on the safe side.

The conclusion that can be drawn from this statistical detour is that the observed frequency distribution of group sizes in a vervet monkey troop is not adequately described by a truncated Poisson distribution.

2.1 Truncated Negative Binomial Distribution

The last column of Table 1.2 gives a theoretical frequency distribution of group sizes obtained by fitting to the observed distribution of vervet sleeping group sizes the density function

$$P(k) = \frac{1}{1 - p^r} \binom{r + k - 1}{k} p^r q^k, \quad \begin{array}{l} k = 1, 2, 3, \ldots \\ q = 1 - p, \\ 0 < p < 1, \\ r > 0, \end{array} \quad (2.1)$$

which is the negative binomial density function truncated at zero (henceforth called the truncated negative binomial distribution). An equivalent recursive definition of this distribution is given by

$$\frac{P(k + 1)}{P(k)} = \frac{rq + qk}{k + 1} = \frac{a + bk}{k + 1}, \quad \begin{array}{l} a = rq > 0 \\ b = q > 0 \\ k = 1, 2, 3, \ldots \end{array} \quad (2.2)$$

and by the requirement that the probabilities sum to 1. The methods used here for fitting the truncated negative binomial to the data are described in the Appendix to this chapter.

Since the agreement between the observed and fitted distributions is good, according to the χ^2 test, this chapter will compare the details of Struhsaker's data with the details of existing models that lead to the truncated negative binomial distribution.

Many probability models lead to the negative binomial distribution (Anscombe 1950; Bliss and Fisher 1953; Irwin 1941; Foster 1952; and see Patil and Joshi 1968, for further references). Most of those models can be easily adapted to produce the truncated form. But only the three models considered below seem interpretable in terms of the vervet monkeys and testable with Struhsaker's data. These models derive the truncated negative binomial distribution as a compound logarithmic distribution (Quenouille 1949), as a compound of Poisson distributions such as Coleman and White proposed, and as a compound of Poisson distributions of the sort proposed by Goodman. Each of these models will be explained in greater detail; the remaining probability models that lead to the negative binomial distribution will be left aside completely.

Quenouille (1949) showed that the sum of a Poisson-distributed number of random variables, each having the logarithmic distribution, has a negative binomial distribution. If the zero value of the Poisson distribution is truncated, then so is the zero value of the negative binomial distribution. G. P. Patil (personal communication, 21 March 1968) suggested that each sleeping group might consist of a truncated Poisson number of subgroups, and that the size of each subgroup might have the logarithmic distribution.

To test that mechanism, it is necessary to have an independent means of defining a subgroup of a sleeping group. One possibility is to suppose that each adult male constitutes the nucleus of a subgroup and that other animals cluster around him. Then the number of adult males per sleeping group should have the truncated Poisson distribution. The analysis of isolates in Chapter 7 shows, however, that several groups had no adult males—in fact, no males at all. Similarly, representatives of every age and sex class were excluded from one group or another. Thus, no age and sex class can be taken to define the nucleus of a subgroup. Patil has suggested (personal communication, 7 May 1968) that location within the grove or tree be used to define subgroups. Unfortunately, Struhsaker's data do not identify such subgroups. Hence, this probability model is at the moment either false or unidentifiable.

The derivation of the negative binomial as a compound Poisson-gamma distribution (explained below) suggests the possibility of analyzing the observed truncated negative binomial distribution into component truncated Poisson distributions, each of which might be described by one of the models of Coleman, White, or Goodman. According to the derivation, if each one of a family of distributions conditional on λ is Poisson, so that

$$P^*(k|\lambda) = \frac{e^{-\lambda}\lambda^k}{k!}, \qquad \begin{array}{l} k = 0, 1, 2, \ldots \\ \lambda > 0 \end{array} \qquad (2.3)$$

and if the parameter λ is distributed over the family according to a gamma (or Pearson Type III) distribution, with density function

$$f^*(\lambda) = \frac{c^r}{\Gamma(r)} e^{-c\lambda}\lambda^{r-1}, \qquad \begin{array}{l} r > 0, 0 < \lambda < \infty, \\ c = p/(1-p), \end{array} \qquad (2.4)$$

then the unconditional probabilities will have the negative binomial distribution (Kendall and Stuart 1958:129–130).

The truncated Poisson distribution (1.1) or

$$P(k|\lambda) = \frac{P^*(k|\lambda)}{1 - P^*(0|\lambda)}, \qquad k = 1, 2, 3, \ldots \qquad (2.5)$$

similarly gives rise to the truncated negative binomial $P(k)$ (2.1) if the mixing density function $f(\lambda)$ is proportional to the gamma density of (2.4) according to

$$f(\lambda) = \frac{f^*(\lambda) \cdot [1 - P(0|\lambda)]}{1 - P(0)}, \qquad \lambda > 0, \qquad (2.6)$$

where $P(0) = p^r/(1 - p^r)$, as in (2.1). Patil (personal communication, 7 May 1968) demonstrated the need for the proportionality factor in (2.6) when going from Poisson to truncated Poisson distributions. (He also pointed out that the truncated negative binomial can arise as a compound distribution from other than the truncated Poisson and modified gamma distributions. However, the models of Coleman, White, and Goodman, give reason to examine the truncated Poisson mixture, and there is no such reason for examining the other possible mixtures, so we will leave them aside.)

We now consider some candidates for the role of the elementary truncated Poisson processes that might compose the observed truncated negative binomial distribution.

2.2 Variation in Time of Mean Group Size

Consider the possibility that, on any particular day, the process of group formation leads to a truncated Poisson distribution of group sizes, but that the parameter λ, which characterizes the process, varies from day to day according to a modified gamma distribution (2.6).

To test this possibility, the mean size of groups on each of the 22 nights observed was calculated. Nine different mean values arose, which are tabulated in Table 2.1. The frequency distributions of group size for the nights with the same mean value were pooled together. Of these nine pooled distributions, eight contained five or more observations. (The number of observations associated with each mean value is also given in Table 2.1.) For each of these eight distributions, the maximum-likelihood estimate of λ (Cohen 1960) and the value of X^2 according to the truncated Poisson variance test (1.4) were found. The eight values of X^2 were then summed to get a value of X^2 that measured whether the observed mean and variance on each day separately were consistent with the hypothesis that the distribution for that day was truncated Poisson. The number of degrees of freedom assigned to this value of X^2 was 81: namely, the number of groups (91) in the list of 22 nights, minus the number of observations discarded (2) from the second day of observation, minus the number of independent estimates of the variance for each of the eight distributions (8). Since the number of degrees of freedom is large, this value of X^2 may be transformed to a standardized normal random variable, $z = 4.69$, which is much too large for the hypothesis of component truncated Poisson processes to be acceptable.

Justification for using the truncated Poisson variance test with only 5 or more observations in a distribution is inferred from sampling experiments with the nontruncated Poisson variance test. Sukhatme (1938) found that as long as $\lambda \geq 2$ and the sample size was 5 or more, the Poisson variance test rejected the null hypothesis of a Poisson distribution with the proper power. (For $\lambda \geq 1$, sample sizes of 15 or more are required for the test to have the proper power.) Since the lowest observed mean group size in Table 2.1 is 2.67,

Table 2.1. Decomposition of the Frequency Distribution of Vervet Group Sizes into Distributions of Nights with Common Mean Sizes

Set of nights	Total number groups	Mean group size	Variance	Maximum likelihood estimate of λ	x^2 equation (1.4)
16, 17, 20, 22	24	2.67	2.41	2.43	27.05
1	5	3.00	2.00	2.82	3.25
18, 21	10	3.20	4.40	3.05	14.59
11, 13	10	3.40	8.93	3.27	27.16
14, 15, 19	12	4.00	6.91	3.92	20.64
3, 4, 9, 10	16	4.25	7.80	4.19	29.43
8, 12	6	5.67	11.07	5.65	9.96
2	2	8.00	18.00	8.00	
5, 6, 7	6	8.50	32.30	8.50	19.03
Total	91				151.11
					df = 81

giving an estimated parameter of 2.43, sample sizes of 5 or more were taken as sufficient.

The possibility that the observed approximately negative binomial distribution arises as a compound time-varying Poisson process thus seems to be excluded.

2.3 Variation Among Animals of Mean Group Size

After presenting his emigration-immigration model, Goodman (1964:191) comments that the same model could lead to the negative binomial distribution if the parameters characterizing the component Poisson processes in it were gamma distributed instead of constant. We will now determine whether, under two interpretations of Goodman's model, the component processes are in fact Poisson distributed.

The model assumes a fixed number n of groups in the system, each of which may at any time contain zero or more individuals. Since the groups continue to exist even when they are empty, it may be more natural to think of them as stations, or booths. A fixed rate is assigned to any transi-

27

tion of an individual from one group to another, from each group to outside the system, and from outside the system to each group.

In the [emigration-immigration] model each group is associated with a particular label (the *j*th group has the label *j*) which we may regard as denoting either the location or purpose of the group or some other identification for the group. This identification is not affected by the size of the group at any given time, by the particular membership at that time, or by the possible temporary "disappearance" of the group . . . For situations where this kind of labeling is not possible, these models are, of course, not to be recommended (Goodman 1964:185).

One possible interpretation of that model would be to identify the *j*th group with the *j*th grove of trees (touching above ground) in the preferred roosting area of the troop. The model would predict that for a given grove, the number of occupants per night would be Poisson distributed. If the mean number varied from one grove to another according to the gamma distribution, the size of sleeping groups would be negative binomially distributed. But the available data do not permit that analysis.

Now we look at two other interpretations. First, each group may be associated with (or labeled by) the most dominant animal in it. This labeling is well defined if the dominance hierarchy is a determinate, linear ordering, which it is in this troop of vervets (Struhsaker 1967c:99). (It makes no difference that very small infants are not really part of the hierarchy, since they never occur alone.) Carrying out this labeling is particularly easy, since Struhsaker has numbered the animals from the top to the bottom of the dominance hierarchy, animal I being highest (Section 1.3). The smallest roman numeral in a group is therefore the label associated with it, and the groups associated with the remaining roman numerals in that group are taken as empty.

In this interpretation, the identity of a group is determined by the most dominant animal in it. That seems reasonable, since all other members of the group must defer to the inclinations of the most dominant member in the allocation of space, food, and sex.

The second interpretation is to label each group by the number of the least dominant animal in it, that is, by the highest roman numeral in the group. Under this procedure, most groups are associated with the youngest infant in them (since they could be dominated by everyone). This assignment is also reasonable in view of the extensive interest in handling and nuzzling infants on the part of all other members of the troop (Struhsaker 1967b:36–40).

Table 2.2 presents the means and variances of the distributions of group sizes under the labelings by most and

Table 2.2. Means and Variances of Sizes of Vervet Groups Characterized by Dominance

Group[a]	Nights observed	Mean size of group	Variance	x^2	df
Most dominant					
I	22	5.77	14.18	51.60	21
II	13	2.62	18.09	83.00	12
III	22	1.55	4.31	58.53	21
IV	22	2.95	9.66	68.69	21
VI	22	1.59	5.30	69.97	21
Least dominant					
XIV	22	2.36	6.34	56.31	21
XV	21	3.38	9.65	57.07	20
XVI[b]	20	7.15	13.29	35.32	19

[a]Only those groups with five or more nonzero observations and mean sizes > 1 are included.

[b]The probability of a larger value of X^2 from the Poisson variance test is < 0.001 in all but this set of groups, where the probability is < 0.025.

least dominant animals. Only those distributions with five or more nonzero observations are included (Sukhatme 1938), and the Poisson variance test is applied. (Those distributions are not truncated at zero, since zero values might be observed on some nights.) In every case the distribution is overdispersed. Hence, under those interpretations of the emigration-immigration model, the sizes of individual groups are not Poisson, and the model does not explain the observed negative binomial distribution.

Appendix to Chapter 2: Fitting the Truncated Negative Binomial

Several methods are available for fitting the truncated negative binomial distribution to given data: the usual method of moments; a method of Rider (1955) involving the first three moments of the observed distribution; and a method of Brass (1958) involving the first two moments and the frequency of 1-counts of the observed distribution. The method of maximum-likelihood estimation, which has been worked out in the case of the nontruncated negative binomial distribution (Bliss and Fisher 1953; Shenton and Myers 1965), is easy to apply here as well. But it leads to equations that are, among the alternative methods, the least attractive for numerical solution. Therefore, this method will not be pursued.

The method of moments requires setting the observed mean and variance equal to the theoretical mean and variance, respectively:

$$\bar{x} = \frac{rq}{p(1 - p^r)} \tag{A2.1}$$

and

$$s^2 = \frac{rq(1 - p^r - rqp^r)}{(1 - p^r)^2 p^2}. \tag{A2.2}$$

The next step is to solve for p and r. Since (A2.1) and (A2.2) are transcendental equations in p and r, solution in closed form is impossible. Approximate numerical solutions may be obtained by two-dimensional Newton-Raphson iteration (Hildebrand 1956:451). That procedure converges only slowly and is computationally much more expensive than that of Rider (1955) or of Brass (1958).

Rider's method is to express the first three moments about zero of the distribution in terms of the two parameters and then to solve for the parameters. The resulting estimators of p and r are

$$\hat{p} = \frac{m_1(m_2 - m_1)}{m_3 m_1 - m_2^2}, \qquad (A2.3)$$

and

$$\hat{r} = \frac{2m_2^2 - m_1(m_2 + m_3)}{m_1(m_3 + m_1) - m_2(m_1 + m_2)}, \qquad (A2.4)$$

where $f(k)$ is the observed frequency of k and the moments m_j are given by

$$m_j = \sum_{k=1}^{\infty} k^j f(k), \qquad j = 0, 1, 2, 3. \qquad (A2.5)$$

Brass's method is to express the transcendental terms in the method of moments in terms of $P(1)$. The resulting estimators of p and r are

$$\hat{p} = \frac{\bar{x}}{s^2} \left(1 - \frac{f(1)}{m_0}\right), \qquad (A2.6)$$

and

$$\hat{r} = \frac{\hat{p} \cdot \bar{x} - f(1)/m_0}{1 - \hat{p}}. \qquad (A2.7)$$

These estimators are consistent but have a bias of order m_0^{-1} that is small for a large number of observations ($m_0 \equiv T$ in Chapter 1). This method of estimation is almost always more efficient than the method of moments and is never less than 96.1 percent as good. Relative to maximum-likelihood estimation, this method is worst as p approaches zero and the distribution is widely spread. Since very low values of p are not observed in the present applications, that is not a problem. Brass gives expressions for the variances and covariance of the two estimators (A2.6) and (A2.7), but those expressions will not be used here since the exact values of the parameters are of less concern than the shape of the distribution.

The χ^2 test measures goodness of fit under the same assumptions made in testing the fit of the truncated Poisson distribution (Section 1.4). But additional caution is necessary in assigning degrees of freedom to calculated values of X^2. As before, let k be the number of cells or classes in the frequency distribution after any pooling has been done.

When ordinary maximum-likelihood estimators are used to find a parameter value from which a theoretical distribution of k cells is generated [as for the zero-truncated Poisson where the estimates of Cohen (1960) are used], then the distribution of X^2 is bounded between a χ^2_{k-1} distribution and a χ^2_{k-2} distribution, where the subscript shows the number of degrees of freedom. As k becomes large, the difference between the two can be ignored. In these cases, if a fit is not rejected assuming $df = k - 2$, it will certainly not be rejected using $df = k - 1$; it is only in cases of marginal fits that the distribution of χ^2_{k-1} needs to be considered. Throughout this study $k - 2$ degrees of freedom have been assigned to values of X^2 calculated against truncated Poisson frequency distributions.

When estimators other than maximum-likelihood or minimum–chi-squared are used, such as Brass's estimators for the truncated negative binomial, it can only be said that X^2 has a distribution with "more" degrees of freedom than $k - \theta - 1$ where θ is the number of parameters estimated. (For the truncated negative binomial, $\theta = 2$.) Hence, if a fit is accepted using the distribution of $\chi^2_{k-\theta-1}$ it would also be accepted using the correct distribution. Cases only marginally rejected (say, at the 0.05 to 0.01 level) using $k - \theta - 1$ degrees of freedom remain doubtful. Throughout this book, $k - 3$ degrees of freedom have been assigned to values of X^2 calculated against truncated negative binomial distributions.

We now compare the fits to observed distributions obtained by using estimators of the method of moments, from Rider (1955) and Brass (1958). Application of the method of moments to Table 1.2 gives $p = 0.43$, $r = 2.73$, and $X^2 = 6.354$ with $df = 9$ (after predicted frequencies have been pooled so that none is less than 1); the probability of a worse fit by chance is between 0.7 and 0.8, which is too large to permit rejection of the assumption that the observations came from a truncated negative binomial distribution. Application of the method of Rider gives $p = 0.38$, $r = 2.16$, and $X^2 = 5.747$ with $df = 10$ (after pooling); the probability of a worse fit by chance is between 0.8 and 0.9, again large. Application of the method of Brass gives $p = 0.34$, $r = 1.74$, and $X^2 = 5.228$ with $df = 10$; the probability of a worse fit by chance is between 0.8 and 0.9. Since the method of Brass gives the best fit of all, the theoretical distribution in Table 1.2 is calculated with the parameters estimated by that method.

We now do the same for the frequency distribution of all observed groups given in Table 1.3. The method of Rider gives $p = 0.37$, $r = 2.12$, and $X^2 = 11.607$ with df $= 11$; the probability of a worse fit by chance is between 0.3 and 0.5, too large to reject the truncated negative binomial. The method of Brass gives $p = 0.35$, $r = 1.92$, and $X^2 = 11.599$ with df $= 11$; the probability of a worse fit by chance is between 0.3 and 0.5. Again, the method of Brass is superior. (The close similarity in the values estimated for p and r in Tables 1.2 and 1.3 shows that, in those data, the effect of any observational bias has been negligible. Whether the groups exhaust the troop, or part of the troop is missing, the parameters estimated for the size distribution are nearly the same.)

On the basis of those and a substantial number of other examples, it seems that the method of Brass generally gives the best fit of the truncated negative binomial distribution to data, as measured by the probability level of the χ^2 test. Henceforth, parameter estimates for that distribution will be based on the method of Brass, unless otherwise specified.

Some combinations of mean and variance are not consistent with the truncated negative binomial distribution. The conditions for the existence of a solution to the moment-matching equations are given by the inequalities (Sampford 1955)

$$q_1 < q_2 < q_3, \tag{A2.8}$$

where

$$q_1 = 1 - \exp\left[-\left(\bar{x} + \frac{s^2}{\bar{x}} - 1\right)\right],$$

$$q_2 = \frac{\bar{x} + (s^2/\bar{x}) - 1}{\bar{x}}, \tag{A2.9}$$

$$q_3 = \log\left(\bar{x} + \frac{s^2}{\bar{x}}\right).$$

If (A2.8) is not satisfied, then no estimates of p and r can satisfy the moment-matching equations exactly; though it would still be possible to obtain estimates of p and r by the method of Brass, the values obtained would be nonsensical.

Therefore, for each frequency distribution the values (A2.9) were calculated, and (A2.8) was checked before the parameters were estimated. For the 22 "good" nights in Table 1.2, $q_1 = 0.99$, $q_2 = 1.33$, and $q_3 = 1.84$. For all the data in Table 1.3, $q_1 = 1.00$, $q_2 = 1.33$, and $q_3 = 1.86$. In both cases (A2.8) is satisfied. Henceforth, the calculated q_i will not be mentioned unless (A2.8) fails to be satisfied.

Further references treating these and other statistical problems in the truncated negative binomial and related distributions may be found in Patil and Joshi (1968).

3.1 Distinguishable Individuals, Indistinguishable Groups

Altmann (1965) suggests a different approach to the process of group formation. He points out the relevance of a classical result in combinatorial theory: the number of ways of distributing N distinguishable (identifiable) individuals into m indistinguishable boxes (or subsets identifiable only by their membership) in such a way that no box is empty is given by $S(N, m)$, the Stirling number of the second kind. The implications of this idea will now be compared with the observations in Table 1.1, which is the frequency distribution of number of groups per night.

For fixed N and values of m within the range from 1 to N, $S(N, m)$ may be taken to define a frequency distribution: namely, $S(N, m)$ is the frequency with which the N individuals fall into exactly m nonempty groups (assuming all distinguishable assignments of individuals to groups to be equiprobable). Thus if p is the lower limit of the range of m ($p \geq 1$) and if q is the upper limit of the range of m ($q \leq N$), then $S(N, m)/\Sigma_{k=p}^{q} S(N, k)$ is the relative frequency of observing m groups. Hence a theoretical mean and variance of number of groups may be calculated and compared with the observed. But to do so requires a choice of N, p, and q.

The most obvious choice is $N = 17$ (the maximum number of individuals in the troop), $p = 1$, and $q = 17$. Table 3.1 gives the observed and predicted means and variances. As a rough measure of agreement between the observed and predicted means, the expression

$$z = \frac{\text{theoretical mean} - \text{observed mean}}{(\text{theoretical variance}/22)^{1/2}} \tag{3.1}$$

is taken to have approximately a standardized normal distribution. Here the observed mean is 4.1364 and 22 is the number of nights of observation. [The expression (3.1) was

previously proposed in a private letter to Stuart A. Altmann from T. V. Narayana, Department of Mathematics,
University of Alberta, Edmonton.] It is apparent (even
without calculating z) that the agreement is poor.

It appears from Table 1.1 that the number of groups observed on any night was restricted to the range from 2 to 6.
If the same restriction is imposed on the theoretical distribution, with $p = 2$ and $q = 6$, correct prediction still is not
obtained.

Table 3.1. Means and Variances of the Number of Vervet Groups Per Night Predicted
by the Combinatorial Models Compared with Observed

Frequency distribution	Range of m	Mean	Variance	z	p	Probability m always in [2,6] [a]
Observed	[2,6]	4.136	1.838			
S(13,m)	[1,13]	5.906	1.340	7.167	b	5.3×10^{-4}
S(13,m)	[2,6]	5.319	0.558	7.426	b	1
S(17,m)	[1,17]	7.231	1.636	11.349	b	1.3×10^{-12}
S(17,m)	[2,6]	5.702	0.273	14.067	b	1
P(13,m)	[1,13]	5.505	5.792	2.667	b	3.1×10^{-4}
P(13,m)	[2,6]	4.286	1.540	0.564		1
P(17,m)	[1,17]	6.616	8.102	4.086	b	1.6×10^{-6}
P(17,m)	[2,6]	4.586	1.387	1.792		1

[a]That is, probability that m would have fallen into the range [2,6] by chance in all 22
observations.
[b]Probability of a z-value of magnitude greater than that observed is less than 0.01.

Another plausible value of N is $N = 13$, since the three
infant monkeys XIV, XV, and XVI never separated from
their mothers and the adult male II left the troop after the
thirteenth night of observation. If animal II is still counted
on the nights during which he was present, the observed
frequency distribution of number of groups per night is
not changed from that given in Table 1.1. The predicted
mean and variance take the values shown in Table 3.1;
again they disagree with the observed distribution, whether
m ranges from 1 to 13 or from 2 to 6.

Thus, in spite of several plausible attempts to patch it up,
Altmann's model of equiprobable allocations of distinguish-

able individuals into indistinguishable groups does not successfully yield even the mean of the observed distribution of number of groups per night.

3.2 Indistinguishable Individuals, Indistinguishable Groups

A model even less sophisticated at first appearance than Altmann's (1965) assumes that individuals are distributed into indistinguishable boxes or groups as if the individuals also were indistinguishable. Thus, in a troop of three animals, the groupings [(I, II), (III)] and [(I), (II, III)] would not be distinguishable under this model, since each grouping consists of one group of one individual and one group of two individuals. Under Altmann's model, the two groupings above would be distinguishable.

Assuming the individuals to be indistinguishable, each grouping of N animals into m groups may be identified with a partition of the number N into m positive summands, or parts, in nondecreasing order. The groupings above, for example, would be identified with the partition of 3 written $1 + 2$. The other possible partitions of 3 are simply 3 itself and $1 + 1 + 1$.

The number of partitions of N into exactly m parts is written $P(N, m)$. Though no closed formula for $P(N, m)$ exists, it may be generated recursively and has been extensively tabulated (Gupta, Gwyther, and Miller 1958). Under the assumption that each partition of N is equiprobable, the numbers $P(N, m)$ define a frequency function for allocations of N animals into m groups, as did $S(N, m)$ in Altmann's model.

Table 3.1 gives the theoretical means and variances predicted by this model for $N = 13$ and $N = 17$, and for ranges of m from 1 to N and from 2 to 6. The model gives quite reasonable agreement in both means and variances when m is restricted to the range from 2 to 6.

In addition to the mean and variance, the full theoretical frequency distribution should agree with the observed. Table 3.2 gives $P(13, m)$, m ranging from 2 to 6, the predictions obtained by normalizing these partition numbers to sum to 22; and the observations repeated from Table 1.1.

Using all five cells and, hence, with df = 4, $X^2 = 4.0953$; a worse fit would have occurred by chance with probability between 0.5 and 0.3. But that fit is hardly convincing because it is based on only 22 observations.

Table 3.2. Frequency Distribution of Number of Vervet Groups Per Night (predictions assume indistinguishable individuals and indistinguishable groups)

Number of groups (m)[a]	$P(13,m)$[b]	$22\,P(13,m)/70$[c]	Observed frequency
2	6	1.89	4
3	14	4.40	2
4	18	5.66	7
5	18	5.66	5
6	14	4.40	4
Total	70	22.01	22

$$x^2 = 4.095$$
$$df = 4$$
$$0.3 < P < 0.5$$

[a]m ranges from 2 to 6.
[b]Number of partitions of 13 into m parts.
[c]Expected number of nights having m sleeping groups.

Another test of the model is a comparison of the observed frequency distribution of group sizes (Table 1.2) with the predicted frequency distribution of size of part in the partitions of N, assuming all partitions equiprobable. Harrison C. White has pointed out privately that this is equivalent to reducing the model from one pertaining to a system of groups (in which the sizes of all groups are specified at once) to one pertaining to a single group (the size of which is chosen from a distribution of group size). While a stronger test of this partition model would be to see if the probabilities of system-states are as predicted, there are not enough data for such a test. There are enough observations of individual group sizes, however, to compare with predictions; and that comparison can at least show if the system-state probabilities are consistent with the observed group size distribution.

Before proceeding to the calculations with the actual

number N of animals in the troop, it seems helpful to work an example supposing there were only $N = 4$ animals in the troop. Here are the ways the troop could split into groups, according to this model:

$1 + 1 + 1 + 1$ (4 groups: 1 animal each)
$1 + 1 + 2$ (3 groups: two isolates and a pair)
$1 + 3$ (2 groups: one isolate and a triple)
$2 + 2$ (2 groups: each a pair)
4 (all together now)

The model assumes that each of those partitions is equi-probable. If any number of groups can occur on a night, then the relative frequency of isolates (parts of size 1) will be 7/12, because there are seven 1's out of 12 groups of all sizes.

If only 2 or 3 groups can form on a night, then we impose the condition that $m = 2$ or $m = 3$; neither a single group nor 4 isolates are permitted. As a result, the relative frequency of isolates will be 3/7; the relative frequency of pairs will also be 3/7; and the relative frequency of triples will be 1/7, by the same counting argument.

For larger values of N, the tedium of counting to predict relative frequencies may be alleviated by mathematics. The frequency of occurrence $R(k, N, m)$ of parts of size k in partitions of N into exactly m parts is given by

$$R(k, N, m) = \sum_{j=1}^{\infty} P(N - jk, m - j), \qquad (3.2)$$

where $P(N, m) = 0$ if either $N \leq 0$ or $m \leq 0$, except that $P(0, 0) = 1$. To obtain the frequency of occurrence of parts of size k given in Table 3.3, $R(k, N, m)$ in (3.2) is summed over m from $m = 2$ to $m = 6$, since that was the observed range of m, the number of groups in any night. The theoretical frequencies of parts of each size given in Table 3.2 were checked by mechanizing the algorithm of Lehmer (1964:26) for the orderly generation of partitions and letting a machine do the counting.

In Table 3.3, the exact distribution for $N = 17$ and $N = 13$ are then normalized to sum to 91, the number of groups observed. The predicted distribution for $N = 17$ is compared with the observations repeated from Table 1.2. The

Table 3.3. Frequency Distribution of Size of Parts in Partitions of N

		Partitions of 17			
Size	Frequency of part [2,6]	Normalized frequency $2 \leqslant m \leqslant 6$	Observed frequency of group size[a]	Normalized frequency $2 \leqslant m \leqslant 8$	Frequency of part [2,8]
1	187	22.9	19	30.0	409
2	145	17.8	14	19.7	269
3	111	13.6	19	12.8	175
4	81	9.9	11	8.5	116
5	60	7.3	7	5.9	81
6	43	5.3	7	4.1	56
7	33	4.0	3	3.0	41
8	24	2.9	2	2.1	29
9	18	2.2	3	1.5	21
10	13	1.6	1	1.1	15
11	10	1.2	2	0.8	11
12	7	0.9	0	0.5	7
13	5	0.6	1	0.4	5
14	3	0.4	2	0.2	3
15	2	1.3 { 0.2	0	1.3 { 0.1	2
16	1	0.1	0	0.1	1
17	0	0	0	0	0
Total	743	90.9	91	90.8	1241
		$x^2 = 8.766$		$x^2 = 16.919$	
		df = 12		df = 11	
		$0.7 < P < 0.8$		$0.1 < P < 0.2$	

		Partitions of 13[b]			
1	94	28.5	27		
2	67	20.3	17		
3	46	14.0	14		
4	30	9.1	9		
5	21	6.4	12		
6	14	4.2	2		
7	10	3.0	4		
8	7	2.1	1		
9	5	1.5	2		
10	3	0.9	0		
11	2	1.8 { 0.6	2		
12	1	0.3	1		
13	0	0	0		
Total	300	90.9	91		
		$x^2 = 8.611$			
		df = 9			
		$0.3 < P < 0.5$			

[a]From Table 1.2.
[b]The presence of XIV, XV, or XVI in a group is ignored.

40

predicted distribution with $N = 13$ is compared with a distribution of group size derived from Struhsaker's list (Section 1.3) by ignoring infants XIV, XV, and XVI as Orwellian unmonkeys (but counting male II while he was present). In both cases, the predicted and observed frequency distributions agree remarkably well, considering the naïveté of the model.

To qualify as an explanation, this model needs independent reasons for restricting m to the range from $p = 2$ to $q = 6$. The elimination of $m = 1$ is an artifact that would be removed if more nights of complete observation were available (Section 1.3); since there is only one arrangement of animals when $m = 1$, the loss makes almost no difference to the shape of the theoretical or observed frequency distributions.

More difficult to account for is the restriction of the number of groups m to values not greater than 6. The last column of Table 3.1 shows the probability, if all partitions of N are equiprobable, that 22 independently observed partitions would all have 2 to 6 components. The probability is so small that chance must be excluded.

Struhsaker (1967c:114–118) has suggested that the size of a vervet troop may be determined by a balance of factors favoring cohesion and factors favoring dispersion; his argument applies as well to the groups within a troop. Increased sensitivity to the approach of predators and the benefits of social grooming and transmitted learning favor cohesion, he argues; but dispersion results in decreased conspicuousness to predators.

To give Struhsaker's arguments quantitative implications, perhaps it is sufficient to observe that the smallest (least conspicuous) group that can still have any of the benefits of sociality is a group of size 2. If the fragmentation of the troop into groups were limited so that the average size of a group were never less than 2 on any night, then in a troop of, effectively, 13 animals, one would never observe more than 6 groups on a night.

By this argument, in a troop of 17 animals, no more than 8 groups on a night would ever be observed. Table 3.3 also gives the frequency distribution of the size of components in partitions of 17 into exactly m components, $2 \leq m \leq 8$.

That distribution, when normalized to sum to 91, is also reasonably close to the observed frequency distribution of group sizes.

This model must be rejected as unsatisfactory, however, for two reasons. The first has to do with the nature of the model's predictions; the second, with its assumptions.

From (3.2) it follows that if $k_1 \leq k_2$, then $R(k_1, N, m) \geq R(k_2, N, m)$; that is, as the size of a part (group) increases, its frequency of occurrence can only decrease. Hence groups of size 2, 3, or more should never occur more frequently than isolates. Struhsaker's data suggest that groups of size 2 or 3 may actually be the mode, while in Lumsden's (1951) data (Section 6.2 here), groups larger than 1 are the mode. Hence, this partition model is qualitatively incapable of accounting for an important characteristic of observed distributions.

Second, the assumption that Nature, and even the monkeys themselves, view members of the troop as indistinguishable is demonstrably false. Struhsaker (1967c:111–112) has shown that some pairs of animals sleep together much more often than they would by chance if all animals were indistinguishable.

Hence, although this model approximates reasonably well the observed distribution of group sizes for one troop of monkeys, it must be rejected as a general model. Section 5.2 will show that this model fails to approximate reasonably well the observed distribution of number of groups in nursery school play, and, thus, may be rejected on grounds of fit as well.

3.3 The Story So Far

Up to this point we have looked at seven theoretical distributions or models and three observed distributions or sets of data. In the remaining chapters, we will examine an additional two theoretical models and their distributions and an additional five sets of observations.

The seven theoretical distributions or models we just considered are the (1) truncated Poisson; (2) truncated negative binomial; (3) compound logarithmic distribution

(Quenouille, Patil); (4) compound truncated Poisson with the parameter varying over time; (5) compound truncated Poisson with the parameter varying over individuals; (6) combinatorial model of Altmann; and (7) random partitions model.

The three observed distributions or sets of data considered are the (1) original data of James, which fit the truncated Poisson distribution; (2) number of groups per night in Struhsaker's vervet data; and (3) sizes of sleeping groups in Struhsaker's vervet data.

Each combination of model or theoretical distribution and data, as presented here, may be characterized in one of four ways: (1) good agreement, +; (2) poor agreement, −; (3) the model or distribution was possibly applicable to the data, but agreement was not checked, 0; (4) the distribution was not applicable to the data, or an analysis of the model was not possible with the details available in the data, x. A matrix which characterizes each combination of model or theoretical distribution and data in one of those four ways appears in Table 8.1. That matrix includes the models and data presented so far as well as the models and data still to come. A scan of the portions of the matrix considered so far suggests that casual or freely forming groups of the kind considered here generally have a truncated Poisson or truncated negative binomial distribution of size, but no interpretable and applicable probability model accounts in detail for how those distributions arise.

Chapter 4 presents a family of linear one-step transition (LOST) models intended to fill the gap. Chapter 5 examines in detail the dynamics in time of free play in a nursery school in order to test the major details of the LOST models. Chapter 6 tries to extend the successes of the LOST models to other data. The last two chapters look at other aspects of casual social groups and evaluate what has been attempted and achieved.

4
Linear
One-Step
Transition
(LOST)
Models

4.1 Closed Systems

Stochastic models . . . where the state in which a group is at the end of any small time interval is contingent not only upon its state at the beginning of that time interval but also upon the actual state of the rest of the system at that time, have been referred to [by Coleman] as "sociological" sorts of models. We would say that models of this kind pertain to *systems* of interdependent groups, whereas models of the kind where the state in which a group is at the end of a particular small time interval is not contingent upon the state of the rest of the system, but only upon the state of that particular group at the beginning of the time period, are models that do *not* pertain to systems of groups (Goodman 1964:171).

The principal difficulty that White (1962) pointed out in the Coleman-James model (1961) was that its defining equations referred not to a system of groups but to a single group. Coleman (1964), without essentially modifying his model, took it therefore as a deterministic approximation to what might be the average behavior of an appropriate stochastic model for a system of groups. White (1962) introduced models of his own that truly pertained to systems of groups, but they were so intractable mathematically that their solution required the introduction of approximations. These approximations, Goodman (1964) pointed out, effectively eliminated the "sociological" aspect of White's models and returned them to the status of Coleman's. Mathematically, the problem in White's models arose from terms in the stochastic differential equations that involved the product of random variables specifying the numbers of groups of particular sizes.

In this chapter, we attempt to avoid these problems by

presenting a family of very simple stochastic models, called the linear one-step transition (LOST) models, for systems of groups. The equilibria predicted by these models are shown to be consistent with most of the available primate and human data. The detailed kinetics the models assume are tested in one case in Chapter 5.

A stochastic model in the narrowest sense would specify the state of the system of groups as a vector giving the number of groups of each size. The dynamics of the model would be Kolmogorov differential equations describing the rate of change over time in the probability of being in each such vector-state. That is the meaning of "stochastic model" in the quotation from Goodman.

Goodman's comments about sociological models of systems of groups apply as well, however, to models that are stochastic in a more relaxed sense, such as Bartlett's (1960:30–33). In models that Bartlett calls stochastic, differential equations specify deterministically rates of change over time in population sizes, and then stochastic terms are added. The defining equations of the LOST models below describe deterministically the rates of change over time in the numbers of groups of each size. For simplicity of exposition, the stochastic terms, whose expectations are all zero, will be added in the Appendix to this chapter. Thus, the equations in this section describe the mean behavior of the stochastic (in the relaxed sense) model of that Appendix.

I will present the defining equations of the model first and an interpretation of them immediately afterwards. Any reader who wishes the help of the interpretation in approaching the equations may skip them now and take them up when the interpretation is discussed.

Let $n_i(t)$ be the number of groups in the system at time t containing i individuals, $i = 1, 2, \ldots$; and let a, b, c, and d be nonnegative constants. Let the model of a closed system be defined by the following equations: for $i = 2, 3, \ldots$,

$$
\begin{aligned}
\frac{dn_i(t)}{dt} = {} & an_{i-1}(t) + b(i-1)n_{i-1}(t) - an_i(t) - bin_i(t) \\
& - cn_i(t) - din_i(t) + cn_{i+1}(t) + d(i+1)n_{i+1}(t)
\end{aligned} \tag{4.1}
$$

and

$$\frac{dn_1(t)}{dt} = -a \sum_{i=1}^{\infty} n_i(t) - an_1(t) - b \sum_{i=1}^{\infty} in_i(t) - bn_1(t)$$
$$+ c \sum_{i=2}^{\infty} n_i(t) + cn_2(t) + d \sum_{i=2}^{\infty} in_i(t) + 2dn_2(t). \tag{4.2}$$

If the total number of groups in the system at time t is $n(t)$ and the total number of individuals is $N(t)$, where

$$n(t) = \sum_{i=1}^{\infty} n_i(t) \quad \text{and} \quad N(t) = \sum_{i=1}^{\infty} in_i(t), \tag{4.3}$$

then (4.1) and (4.2) imply, for all t, by simple summation, that

$$\sum_{i=2}^{\infty} \frac{dn_i(t)}{dt} = an_1(t) + bn_1(t) - cn_2(t) - 2dn_2(t) \tag{4.4}$$

and

$$\frac{dN(t)}{dt} = 0. \tag{4.5}$$

Thus, the constancy of the number of individuals in the system is a consequence of the defining equations, as is desired in a closed system.

The following interpretation may make (4.1) and (4.2) more plausible. Consider the number of groups of size i, $i = 2, 3, \ldots$. Equation (4.1) says that the number of such groups will increase in a short interval of time, either because of the arrival of individuals at groups of size 1 less (first two terms of the right member) or because of the departure of individuals from groups of size 1 more (last two terms of the right member). Moreover, the rate of arrival will be the sum of two rates, one proportional to the number of groups of size 1 less (an_{i-1}) and the second proportional to the number of individuals in groups of size 1 less $[b(i-1)n_{i-1}]$. Similarly, departures will occur when individuals leave groups of size 1 more at a rate proportional only to the number of such groups ("group expulsion") and not to the number of individuals in such groups (cn_{i+1}). Or they will occur when individuals make independent decisions to leave a group and hence do so at a total rate proportional to the number of individuals in groups of that size $[d(i + 1)n_{i+1}]$. The same equation (4.1) indicates that the number of groups of size i will decrease, on the other hand, when the same rates of arrival and departure are at work on groups of size i (the middle four terms of the right member).

The rate of change of the number of isolates, or groups of size 1, is specified separately in (4.2). The number of isolates will decrease by 1 every time an isolate joins a group of size 2 or greater; but when 1 isolate joins another to form a pair, 2 isolates are eliminated, hence the extra terms $-an_1$ and $-bn_1$. So an isolated individual is attractive both as a group (of size 1) and as a member of a (potentially larger) group. Similarly, the number of isolates will increase by one every time an individual leaves a group of size 3 or larger; but when a pair splits up, 2 isolates are created, hence the extra terms cn_2 and $2dn_2$.

This interpretation of (4.1) and (4.2) views the system of groups from outside and describes flow patterns. A more "psychological" interpretation, taking the point of view of an average individual in the system, is also possible. Loosely speaking, if I am an individual in the system and am an isolate, then the equations indicate that I want to join a group or another isolate either because I feel like joining a group qua group (hence with an average probability in the next small interval of time proportional to the number of groups) or because I am attracted by an individual in some group (hence with an average probability in the next small interval of time proportional to the number of individuals in groups). But—and this is a counterintuitive feature of the model—because the arrival terms an_i and bin_i, $i \geq 2$, are independent of the number of isolates in the system, according to this psychological interpretation, my propensity as an isolate in the system to join a group is actually inversely proportional to the number of isolates presently in the system. That is, if there were twice as many isolates but the same number of triples, say, then my inclination to join a triple would have to average one-half of what it is now, in order to guarantee a constant rate of arrival to triples.

On the other hand, if I am an individual in the system and am already in a group of size ≥ 2, then the group may

47

eject me at a rate independent of the number of isolates in the system and of the size of the group; or I may simply feel like getting out of the group (independently of the number of isolates in the system) and hence contribute to the departures occurring at a rate proportional to the number of individuals in groups of each size. Whereas the latter departures (at the rate din_i) can be explained on the basis of assumptions about independent individual behavior, the former departures (at the rate cn_i) cannot, for that term assumes that an individual in a group of size $2i$ is only one half as likely to leave the group as an individual in a group of size i. Upon leaving a group of size ≥ 2, I must join, however briefly, the pool of isolates; I cannot go directly to another large group.

Under those interpretations, the parameter a may be thought of loosely as specifying the attractiveness of groups including isolates qua groups, hence a group arrival rate; b may be thought of as specifying the attractiveness of joining individuals in groups, or an individual arrival rate; c, a group departure rate; and d, an individual departure rate.

What is novel, and far from obviously true, in this model is the assumption that the arrival rates for groups larger than 2 and the departure rates for groups larger than 1 are all independent of the number of isolates in the system at the time. White's (1962) models typically include a term of the form $n_1 n_i$, $i \geq 2$, so that if there are no isolates at a particular instant, no groups of size i are joined by individuals. The model just presented, however, says that the number of arrivals in a short time period to groups of size i, when divided by the number of such groups at the beginning of the interval, should be a linear function of i with slope b and, extrapolated to $i = 0$, with intercept a; similarly for departures—all independently of the number of isolates in the system at the time. It is obviously impossible for this condition to be satisfied if the system ever reaches a state where $n_1 = 0$; that is, if no individuals in the system are isolates, since no arrivals to groups of size greater than 1 would then be possible. Thus, the defining equations must be taken as approximate in the vicinity of the states where $n_1 = 0$. And in order for them to hold, the departure parameters must be large enough relative to the arrival parameters to guarantee in each short time interval the isolates required for the arrivals of the next interval.

If the true dynamics of systems of freely forming groups is described by some nonlinear model whose equations of change involve products of the form $n_1 n_i$, and if the parameters of the system lead to an abundance of isolates in comparison with the numbers of larger groups, then one would expect the rate-limiting factor in each such product to be the number of larger groups. Hence, in a system with a large number of isolates, one could expect to approximate nonlinear dynamics with simple linear dynamics like those of the LOST models. On the other hand, if isolates were in short supply, one would expect them to be the rate-limiting factor, and equations like those of the LOST models would be inadequate approximations.

With the nursery school data of Chapter 5 and with the additional equilibrium distributions in Chapter 6, it is impossible to test whether the LOST models give poor predictions when isolates are rare, because isolates are abundant in all of the situations. But the assumption of the linearity of the number of arrivals to and departures from groups of size i (undefined for $i = 0$) is such a strong one that it ought to be easily testable empirically.

Another virtue of assuming such linearity is that the frequency distribution of group sizes observed in the system is then directly proportional to the probability distribution of the size of a single group. Therefore, observed frequency distributions of the sizes of single groups, such as that derived from Struhsaker's data, can be legitimately compared with the theoretical distribution of group sizes in the system as a whole. (Section 4.2 gives the details of this argument.)

After the development, application, and testing of the LOST models below had been completed, it was privately pointed out to me that the LOST models are formally similar to the two-way contagious Poisson model of Coleman (1964:326–332), except for the truncation at zero and the terms in the LOST models involving the parameter c (which, it will appear, must be taken to be zero).

49

The correspondence of the LOST parameters with those of the two-way contagious Poisson is $a = \alpha'$, $b = \gamma'$, and $d = \beta'$. In spite of the formal similarity, there is the same difference in substance between the two-way contagious Poisson and the LOST models as between the model of Coleman and James (1961) and White's (1962) models: the variables in the equations of the two-way contagious Poisson are the probabilities of states of a single aggregation or group, while the variables of the LOST models refer to "sociological" systems of interacting groups. (Coleman's two-way contagious Poisson, closely related to a contagious model of Irwin (1941), seems more appropriate to the data on bottled mammals presented in Section 8.1.)

4.2 Equilibrium Solution

The process specified by the model is said to be in equilibrium if, for all i,

$$\frac{dm_i}{dt} = 0, \tag{4.6}$$

where

$$m_i = \lim_{t \to \infty} E[n_i(t)]. \tag{4.7}$$

The limits m_i and the equilibrium are assumed to exist and their properties will now be determined. (The notation of (4.7) should not be confused with the raw moments defined in (A2.5).)

If m is the limiting expected value of $n(t)$, then replacing n by m everywhere in (4.4) and setting the left member to zero gives

$$\frac{m_2}{m_1} = \frac{a + b}{c + 2d}. \tag{4.8}$$

Applying the same procedure to (4.1) successively for $i = 2, 3, \ldots$ gives

$$\frac{m_{i+1}}{m_i} = \frac{a + bi}{c + d(i + 1)}, \tag{4.9}$$

which includes (4.8) as the case for $i = 1$. By appropriate choice of the time scale, which makes no difference at equilibrium, we may take $d = 1$. (Equivalently, the numerator and denominator of (4.9) are divided by d.) Thus for $i = 1, 2, \ldots,$

$$\frac{f(i+1)}{f(i)} = \frac{m_{i+1}}{m_i} = \frac{a+bi}{c+i+1}, \qquad (4.10)$$

where $f(i) = m_i/m$ is the fraction of groups at equilibrium that are of size i. This is not necessarily the same as the expected fraction of groups that are of size i. To find $f(i)$, expectations are taken first and the quotient is formed second. This procedure corresponds to the observed relative frequency of groups of size i, since the system is assumed to be at equilibrium at the time of observation.

The bilinear, first-order difference equation (4.10), plus a normalizing condition

$$\sum_{i=1}^{\infty} f(i) = 1, \qquad (4.11)$$

define a family of frequency functions. Happily, the theory of this family has been developed from the defining difference equation by Katz (1945, 1946, 1965). Hence in quoting results from him I will not offer proof.

In the following special cases, let $a > 0$ everywhere. We first consider the possibility $c = 0$ and then the possibility $c \neq 0$.

If $c = 0$ and $b = 0$, $f(i)$ is the density function of a zero-truncated Poisson distribution with parameter $\lambda = a$. Thus, under the interpretation above, if individuals join groups only because of their attractiveness qua groups and leave them for individual reasons only, then the frequency distribution of group sizes will be exactly that found in most of James's data on humans. The model of a closed system presented here is obviously inappropriate to a situation as open as that of pedestrians passing on a sidewalk (see the next section for an extension to open systems), but it may be proper for the observations of children on playgrounds if the set of children at play is fixed during the period of observation.

If $c = 0$ and $b > 0$, $f(i)$ is the density function of a truncated negative binomial distribution with $a = rq$ and $b = q$. In fact (4.10) then reproduces (2.2). Under the interpretation above, if individuals also join groups because of the attractiveness of individuals in them, then the frequency distribution of group sizes will be that found in Struhsaker's data on vervet monkeys.

If $c = 0$ and $b < 0$, $f(i)$ is the density function of a truncated binomial distribution. But the case $b < 0$ is uninterpretable in terms of the defining equations of the model; hence, an observed truncated binomial distribution would require another model. (No truncated binomial distribution has been observed among the social data reviewed here.)

If $c \neq 0$, consider the variable z defined by $z = i + c$. If g is the frequency function of z, then from (4.10),

$$\frac{g(z+1)}{g(z)} = \frac{a + b(z - c)}{c + (z - c) + 1} = \frac{a' + bz}{z + 1}, \qquad (4.12)$$

where $a' = a - bc$. Accordingly, z has a truncated Poisson or truncated negative binomial distribution as $b = 0$ or $b > 0$, and i has a translated Poisson or negative binomial distribution, starting with the value $i = 1 - c$ and moving to the right. [Katz 1945 proves this directly from the defining equation (4.10).] Thus, if c is positive, the lowest observed values of i will be less than 1 and, conceivably, negative. In this situation where i represents the size of groups, such values would be impossible; hence, if the model is correct, c should never be positive. If the model presented here is correctly interpreted, it makes no sense for c to be negative. Thus, c should always be 0.

In conclusion, the model is consistent only with truncated Poisson or truncated negative binomial distributions. The distributions are specified by two parameters, a and b. This is double the number of parameters used by Coleman, White, and Goodman. For describing some sets of data that have only four, five, or six values, this increase constitutes a very considerable gain in freedom, and improved success with such sets of data is hardly surprising. The two-parameter LOST model is really tested only by sets of equilibrium data with larger numbers of values (such as Struhsaker's) and by detailed dynamic data.

Ideally, in addition to the equilibrium mean of $n_i(t)$, one would like to know its full distribution, or at least some higher moments. I am unable to calculate exactly even the variance, so the full exploration of this model remains an open mathematical problem.

The Appendix to this chapter attempts to approximate the equilibrium variance of $n_i(t)$ and, on the basis of the best approximation obtainable there, to justify the use of the χ^2 test in measuring the goodness of fit of group size distributions to the predicted equilibrium distribution.

4.3 Open Systems

The difference equations (4.8) and (4.9), which lead to the truncated Poisson and truncated negative binomial distributions, depend on the defining equation (4.1) and on the equation (4.4) for $d[n(t) - n_1(t)]/dt$, which follows from (4.1). Hence the form and variance of the equilibrium distribution depend only on (4.1) and are independent of the function specified for $dn_1(t)/dt$, as long as that function vanishes as the system goes to equilibrium.

Suppose, instead of (4.2), that isolates follow exactly the same law as larger groups, namely (4.1), except for those terms of (4.1) that would refer to groups of size zero (which do not exist). Thus, suppose

$$\frac{dn_1(t)}{dt} = -an_1 - bn_1 + cn_2 + 2dn_2. \qquad (4.13)$$

In effect, isolates in the system are attracted directly only by other isolates in the system, either as individuals or as single-member groups but not by larger groups. Isolates are produced only by the fission of pairs. All individuals leaving groups of size greater than 2 quit the system, and those joining groups of size greater than 1 join this system from outside.

In combination (4.1) and (4.13) imply

$$\frac{dn(t)}{dt} = 0 \qquad (4.14)$$

and

$$\frac{dN(t)}{dt} = an(t) + bN(t) - c[n(t) - n_1(t)]$$
$$- d[N(t) - n_1(t)]. \qquad (4.15)$$

Hence, the system has a fixed number of groups (counting isolates as groups of size 1). In this case, $E(n_i/n) = E(n_i)/n$, and the fraction of groups at equilibrium that are of size i equals the expected fraction of groups that are of size i.

The change in the total number of individuals $N(t)$ over time is described by (4.15), which says that individuals from outside enter the system and leave it by the same law they follow regarding a group of any size. Since the equations that lead at equilibrium to a truncated Poisson or truncated negative binomial distribution of group sizes still hold, the model as modified may apply to some of the obviously open systems from which some of the human data were obtained.

Other laws for $dn_1(t)/dt$ would lead to different expressions for $dn(t)/dt$ and $dN(t)/dt$. However, they would preserve (4.1) and, hence, would preserve the same equilibrium distribution.

In another interpretation of the model, suggested by a different model and by data of Horvath and Foster (1963), the theoretical individuals could be viewed as nations and the theoretical groups as alliances for war. The consequences of this interpretation will be reviewed in Section 6.4.

4.4 Time Scale: Approach to Equilibrium

The equilibria predicted by the linear one-step transition models are independent of the time scale. The location and spread of the equilibrial distributions depend only on the ratios a/d and b/d. But in testing the details of the mixing processes proposed by these models, it is necessary to have some reasonable ideas, first, about the absolute time scale, and second, about how close to equilibrium the system may be expected to be if the parameters a, b, and d measured on that time scale have the values observed.

In the case of the vervet monkey troop, I assume that the mixing process goes on all day when the troop is on the ground, many monkeys changing groups within each hour. The composition of the sleeping groups at night is assumed to be a freezing, like a snapshot, of that mixing process. Each morning, the mixing is assumed to continue where it left off the night before.

In studying children at play, a time unit would have to be chosen that was long enough to allow at least one transition to take place within it and short enough so that it would be sufficient to record the state of the system (number of groups of each size) only once, at the beginning of each unit. Such a unit might be, for example, 30 seconds or a minute, depending on the tempo of play.

Given estimates of the parameters a, b, and d and an initial frequency distribution of group sizes, it is possible to determine the rapidity of approach to apparent equilibrium either by simulation of the defining equations as stochastic processes or by numerical solution of the defining equations interpreted deterministically. The latter approach reveals the mean behavior of a large number of identical stochastic systems obeying these equations, and it eliminates the variability in $n_i(t)$ for given t. Consequently, if this deterministic approximation fails to reach apparent equilibrium by a certain time t, it is safe to conclude that the stochastic system will not reliably appear equilibrial by that time. If the deterministic system does look equilibrial and if the variance $\mathrm{Var}[n_i(t)]$ is small, then the stochastic system will also look equilibrial. The remainder of this section describes the approach to equilibrium of open and closed systems obeying the defining equations interpreted deterministically.

The family of equations (4.1) is infinite. Machine computation can handle only a finite number, say M, of equations simultaneously. (M is any finite number, not the limit of $E[N(t)]$ as above.) Therefore, we approximate (4.1) by the system

$$\frac{dn_i(t)}{dt} = a[n_{i-1}(t) - n_i(t)] + b[(i-1)n_{i-1}(t) - in_i(t)]$$
$$- d[in_i(t) - (i+1)n_{i+1}(t)], \quad i = 2, 3, \ldots, M. \quad (4.16)$$

55

We require that

$$n_{M+1}(t) = 0 \tag{4.17}$$

on the assumption that, for reasonable values of a, b, and d, the number $n_{M+1}(t)$ of groups of size $M + 1$ will always be so close to zero that this approximation introduces negligible error. To compute the behavior of a closed system (with, ideally, a fixed number of individuals), we approximate (4.2) by

$$\frac{dn_1(t)}{dt} = -a \sum_{i=1}^{M} n_i(t) - an_1(t) - b \sum_{i=1}^{M} in_i(t)$$
$$- bn_1(t) + d \sum_{i=2}^{M} in_i(t) + 2dn_2(t). \tag{4.18}$$

For an open system (with, ideally, a fixed number of groups) the behavior of isolates, as in (4.13), is specified by

$$\frac{dn_1(t)}{dt} = -an_1(t) - bn_1(t) + 2dn_2(t). \tag{4.19}$$

Terms involving c are absent from these equations, since c must be zero.

The total number $n(t)$ of groups at time t and the total number $N(t)$ of individuals at time t are defined by (4.3), with all terms after the Mth in the summations being zero.

For closed systems it then follows that

$$\frac{dn(t)}{dt} = -a[n(t) + n_M(t)] - b[N(t) + Mn_M(t)]$$
$$- d[N(t) - n_1(t)], \tag{4.20}$$

and

$$\frac{dN(t)}{dt} = -[(M + 1)(a + bM)]n_M(t). \tag{4.21}$$

Hence, in a numerical approximation of this system, the total number of individuals will not be constant but will decrease at a rate proportional to the number of groups of size M, the largest size considered.

For open systems,

$$\frac{dn(t)}{dt} = -(a + bM)n_M(t) \tag{4.22}$$

and

$$\begin{aligned}\frac{dN(t)}{dt} = {} &an(t) - a(M+1)n_M(t) + bN(t) \\ &- bM(M+1)n_M(t) - dN(t) + dn_1(t) \\ &+ 2dMn_M(t).\end{aligned} \tag{4.23}$$

Hence, in a numerical approximation of an open system that ideally has a fixed number of groups, the total number of groups will actually decrease at a rate proportional to the number of groups of size M. The number of individuals may increase or decrease depending on the sign of the right side of (4.23).

The equations for the closed and for the open systems were solved numerically using an algorithm, HAMING, written in Fortran IV by Donald G. M. Anderson of the Aiken Computation Laboratory, Harvard University. The routine solves an arbitrary set of first-order differential equations by using the Hamming predictor-corrector algorithm. Starting values for the solution are obtained by Picard iteration, which demands a mesh size (Δt) small enough for the iteration to converge. A mesh size of 1/32 (in the same units of time as a, b, and d) was found to be sufficiently small for all the present computations.

The routine was supplied with the equations specifying either the closed or open system, values for the parameters a, b, and d (unit = time^{-1}) and an initial frequency distribution of group sizes (for example, 100 isolates and no other groups). The number of equations was fixed at $M = 9$, so that no groups of size 10 or larger were considered. The routine yielded the number of groups of each size at selected times after $t = 0$ up to $t = 20$. The total number of groups $n(t)$ and total number $N(t)$ of individuals at that instant were printed along with each time and frequency distribution. Tables 4.1, 4.2, 4.3, and 4.4 present the results of sample calculations. Tables 4.1 and 4.2 describe the behavior of a closed system satisfying (4.16) and (4.18). Tables 4.3 and 4.4 describe the behavior of an open system satisfying (4.16) and (4.19).

Table 4.1. Calculated Behavior of a Closed System of Groups According to the
LOST Model[a]

Number of groups of each size

Time	1	2	3	4	5	6	7	8	9	Total groups	Total indiv.
0.0000	100.0	0.0	0.0	0.0	0.0	0.0	0.0	0.0	0.0	100.0	100.0
0.0313	94.6	2.6	0.0	0.0	0.0	0.0	0.0	0.0	0.0	97.3	100.0
0.0625	89.8	4.8	0.2	0.0	0.0	0.0	0.0	0.0	0.0	94.8	100.0
0.0938	85.4	6.7	0.4	0.0	0.0	0.0	0.0	0.0	0.0	92.5	100.0
0.1250	81.4	8.4	0.6	0.0	0.0	0.0	0.0	0.0	0.0	90.4	100.0
0.1563	77.7	9.8	0.8	0.1	0.0	0.0	0.0	0.0	0.0	88.4	100.0
0.1875	74.4	11.0	1.1	0.1	0.0	0.0	0.0	0.0	0.0	86.6	100.0
0.2188	71.4	12.0	1.4	0.1	0.0	0.0	0.0	0.0	0.0	84.9	100.0
0.2500	68.6	12.8	1.6	0.2	0.0	0.0	0.0	0.0	0.0	83.3	100.0
0.2813	66.1	13.6	1.9	0.2	0.0	0.0	0.0	0.0	0.0	81.8	100.0
0.3125	63.8	14.2	2.2	0.3	0.0	0.0	0.0	0.0	0.0	80.5	100.0
0.3438	61.6	14.7	2.4	0.3	0.0	0.0	0.0	0.0	0.0	79.2	100.0
0.3750	59.7	15.2	2.7	0.4	0.1	0.0	0.0	0.0	0.0	78.0	100.0
0.4063	57.9	15.6	2.9	0.5	0.1	0.0	0.0	0.0	0.0	76.9	100.0
0.4375	56.3	15.9	3.1	0.5	0.1	0.0	0.0	0.0	0.0	75.9	100.0
0.4688	54.7	16.1	3.4	0.6	0.1	0.0	0.0	0.0	0.0	74.9	100.0
0.5000	53.3	16.4	3.6	0.7	0.1	0.0	0.0	0.0	0.0	74.0	100.0
0.5313	52.0	16.5	3.7	0.7	0.1	0.0	0.0	0.0	0.0	73.2	100.0
0.5625	50.8	16.7	3.9	0.8	0.1	0.0	0.0	0.0	0.0	72.4	100.0
0.5938	49.7	16.8	4.1	0.8	0.2	0.0	0.0	0.0	0.0	71.7	100.0
0.6250	48.7	16.9	4.2	0.9	0.2	0.0	0.0	0.0	0.0	71.0	100.0
0.6563	47.8	17.0	4.4	1.0	0.2	0.0	0.0	0.0	0.0	70.3	100.0
0.6875	46.9	17.0	4.5	1.0	0.2	0.0	0.0	0.0	0.0	69.7	100.0
0.7188	46.1	17.0	4.7	1.1	0.2	0.0	0.0	0.0	0.0	69.2	100.0
0.7500	45.3	17.1	4.8	1.1	0.3	0.1	0.0	0.0	0.0	68.6	100.0
0.7813	44.6	17.1	4.9	1.2	0.3	0.1	0.0	0.0	0.0	68.1	100.0
0.8125	44.0	17.1	5.0	1.3	0.3	0.1	0.0	0.0	0.0	67.7	100.0
0.8438	43.4	17.1	5.1	1.3	0.3	0.1	0.0	0.0	0.0	67.2	100.0
0.8750	42.8	17.1	5.2	1.3	0.3	0.1	0.0	0.0	0.0	66.8	100.0
0.9063	42.3	17.0	5.2	1.4	0.3	0.1	0.0	0.0	0.0	66.4	100.0
0.9375	41.8	17.0	5.3	1.4	0.4	0.1	0.0	0.0	0.0	66.0	100.0
0.9688	41.4	17.0	5.4	1.5	0.4	0.1	0.0	0.0	0.0	65.7	100.0
1.0000	40.9	16.9	5.4	1.5	0.4	0.1	0.0	0.0	0.0	65.4	100.0
1.0625	40.2	16.9	5.6	1.6	0.4	0.1	0.0	0.0	0.0	64.8	100.0
1.1250	39.5	16.8	5.7	1.7	0.5	0.1	0.0	0.0	0.0	64.2	100.0
1.1875	38.9	16.7	5.7	1.7	0.5	0.1	0.0	0.0	0.0	63.8	100.0
1.2500	38.4	16.6	5.8	1.8	0.5	0.1	0.0	0.0	0.0	63.3	100.0
1.3125	38.0	16.6	5.9	1.8	0.5	0.1	0.0	0.0	0.0	63.0	100.0
1.3750	37.6	16.5	5.9	1.9	0.6	0.2	0.0	0.0	0.0	62.6	100.0
1.4375	37.2	16.4	6.0	1.9	0.6	0.2	0.0	0.0	0.0	62.3	100.0
1.5000	36.9	16.3	6.0	2.0	0.6	0.2	0.0	0.0	0.0	62.0	100.0
1.5625	36.6	16.3	6.0	2.0	0.6	0.2	0.1	0.0	0.0	61.8	100.0
1.6250	36.4	16.2	6.0	2.0	0.6	0.2	0.1	0.0	0.0	61.6	100.0
1.6875	36.2	16.1	6.1	2.1	0.7	0.2	0.1	0.0	0.0	61.4	99.9
1.7500	36.0	16.1	6.1	2.1	0.7	0.2	0.1	0.0	0.0	61.2	99.9
1.8125	35.8	16.0	6.1	2.1	0.7	0.2	0.1	0.0	0.0	61.0	99.9
1.8750	35.6	16.0	6.1	2.1	0.7	0.2	0.1	0.0	0.0	60.9	99.9
1.9375	35.5	15.9	6.1	2.1	0.7	0.2	0.1	0.0	0.0	60.7	99.9
2.0000	35.4	15.9	6.1	2.2	0.7	0.2	0.1	0.0	0.0	60.6	99.9
2.1250	35.2	15.8	6.1	2.2	0.7	0.2	0.1	0.0	0.0	60.4	99.9
2.2500	35.0	15.8	6.2	2.2	0.8	0.2	0.1	0.0	0.0	60.2	99.9
2.3750	34.9	15.7	6.2	2.2	0.8	0.3	0.1	0.0	0.0	60.1	99.8
2.5000	34.8	15.7	6.2	2.2	0.8	0.3	0.1	0.0	0.0	60.0	99.8
2.6250	34.7	15.6	6.2	2.3	0.8	0.3	0.1	0.0	0.0	59.9	99.8
2.7500	34.6	15.6	6.2	2.3	0.8	0.3	0.1	0.0	0.0	59.8	99.8
2.8750	34.5	15.6	6.2	2.3	0.8	0.3	0.1	0.0	0.0	59.7	99.7
3.0000	34.5	15.5	6.2	2.3	0.8	0.3	0.1	0.0	0.0	59.7	99.7
3.2500	34.4	15.5	6.2	2.3	0.8	0.3	0.1	0.0	0.0	59.5	99.7
3.5000	34.3	15.5	6.2	2.3	0.8	0.3	0.1	0.0	0.0	59.5	99.6
3.7500	34.3	15.4	6.2	2.3	0.8	0.3	0.1	0.0	0.0	59.4	99.5
4.0000	34.2	15.4	6.2	2.3	0.8	0.3	0.1	0.0	0.0	59.3	99.5
4.5000	34.2	15.4	6.2	2.3	0.8	0.3	0.1	0.0	0.0	59.2	99.4
5.0000	34.1	15.4	6.1	2.3	0.8	0.3	0.1	0.0	0.0	59.2	99.3
6.0000	34.0	15.3	6.1	2.3	0.8	0.3	0.1	0.0	0.0	59.0	99.0
7.0000	33.9	15.3	6.1	2.3	0.8	0.3	0.1	0.0	0.0	58.9	98.8
8.0000	33.9	15.3	6.1	2.3	0.8	0.3	0.1	0.0	0.0	58.7	98.6
9.0000	33.8	15.2	6.1	2.3	0.8	0.3	0.1	0.0	0.0	58.6	98.3
10.0000	33.7	15.2	6.1	2.3	0.8	0.3	0.1	0.0	0.0	58.5	98.1
11.0000	33.6	15.2	6.1	2.3	0.8	0.3	0.1	0.0	0.0	58.3	97.9
12.0000	33.5	15.1	6.0	2.3	0.8	0.3	0.1	0.0	0.0	58.2	97.6
13.0000	33.5	15.1	6.0	2.3	0.8	0.3	0.1	0.0	0.0	58.1	97.4
14.0000	33.4	15.0	6.0	2.3	0.8	0.3	0.1	0.0	0.0	57.9	97.2
15.0000	33.3	15.0	6.0	2.2	0.8	0.3	0.1	0.0	0.0	57.8	97.0
16.0000	33.2	15.0	6.0	2.2	0.8	0.3	0.1	0.0	0.0	57.6	96.7
17.0000	33.2	14.9	6.0	2.2	0.8	0.3	0.1	0.0	0.0	57.5	96.5
18.0000	33.1	14.9	6.0	2.2	0.8	0.3	0.1	0.0	0.0	57.4	96.3
19.0000	33.0	14.9	5.9	2.2	0.8	0.3	0.1	0.0	0.0	57.2	96.1
20.0000	32.9	14.8	5.9	2.2	0.8	0.3	0.1	0.0	0.0	57.1	95.8

[a] $M = 9$, $a = 0.6000$, $b = 0.3000$, $d = 1.0000$.

58

Table 4.2. Calculated Behavior of a Closed System of Groups According to the LOST Model[a]

	Number of groups of each size									Total groups	Total indiv.
Time	1	2	3	4	5	6	7	8	9		
0.0000	100.0	0.0	0.0	0.0	0.0	0.0	0.0	0.0	0.0	100.0	100.0
0.0313	89.8	4.8	0.2	0.0	0.0	0.0	0.0	0.0	0.0	94.8	100.0
0.0625	81.4	8.4	0.6	0.0	0.0	0.0	0.0	0.0	0.0	90.4	100.0
0.0938	74.4	11.0	1.1	0.1	0.0	0.0	0.0	0.0	0.0	86.6	100.0
0.1250	68.6	12.8	1.6	0.2	0.0	0.0	0.0	0.0	0.0	83.3	100.0
0.1563	63.8	14.2	2.2	0.3	0.0	0.0	0.0	0.0	0.0	80.5	100.0
0.1875	59.7	15.2	2.7	0.4	0.1	0.0	0.0	0.0	0.0	78.0	100.0
0.2188	56.3	15.9	3.1	0.5	0.1	0.0	0.0	0.0	0.0	75.9	100.0
0.2500	53.3	16.4	3.6	0.7	0.1	0.0	0.0	0.0	0.0	74.0	100.0
0.2813	50.8	16.7	3.9	0.8	0.1	0.0	0.0	0.0	0.0	72.4	100.0
0.3125	48.7	16.9	4.2	0.9	0.2	0.0	0.0	0.0	0.0	71.0	100.0
0.3438	46.9	17.0	4.5	1.0	0.2	0.0	0.0	0.0	0.0	69.7	100.0
0.3750	45.3	17.1	4.8	1.1	0.3	0.1	0.0	0.0	0.0	68.6	100.0
0.4063	44.0	17.1	5.0	1.3	0.3	0.1	0.0	0.0	0.0	67.7	100.0
0.4375	42.8	17.1	5.2	1.3	0.3	0.1	0.0	0.0	0.0	66.8	100.0
0.4688	41.8	17.0	5.3	1.4	0.4	0.1	0.0	0.0	0.0	66.0	100.0
0.5000	40.9	16.9	5.4	1.5	0.4	0.1	0.0	0.0	0.0	65.4	100.0
0.5313	40.2	16.9	5.6	1.6	0.4	0.1	0.0	0.0	0.0	64.8	100.0
0.5625	39.5	16.8	5.7	1.7	0.5	0.1	0.0	0.0	0.0	64.2	100.0
0.5938	38.9	16.8	5.7	1.7	0.5	0.1	0.0	0.0	0.0	63.8	100.0
0.6250	38.4	16.6	5.8	1.8	0.5	0.1	0.0	0.0	0.0	63.3	100.0
0.6563	38.0	16.6	5.9	1.8	0.5	0.1	0.0	0.0	0.0	63.0	100.0
0.6875	37.6	16.5	5.9	1.9	0.6	0.2	0.0	0.0	0.0	62.6	100.0
0.7188	37.2	16.4	6.0	1.9	0.6	0.2	0.0	0.0	0.0	62.3	100.0
0.7500	36.9	16.3	6.0	2.0	0.6	0.2	0.0	0.0	0.0	62.0	100.0
0.7813	36.6	16.3	6.0	2.0	0.6	0.2	0.1	0.0	0.0	61.8	100.0
0.8125	36.4	16.2	6.0	2.0	0.6	0.2	0.2	0.0	0.0	61.6	100.0
0.8438	36.2	16.1	6.1	2.1	0.7	0.2	0.1	0.0	0.0	61.4	99.9
0.8750	36.0	16.1	6.1	2.1	0.7	0.2	0.1	0.0	0.0	61.2	99.9
0.9063	35.8	16.0	6.1	2.1	0.7	0.2	0.1	0.0	0.0	61.0	99.9
0.9375	35.6	16.0	6.1	2.1	0.7	0.2	0.1	0.0	0.0	60.9	99.9
0.9688	35.5	15.9	6.1	2.1	0.7	0.2	0.1	0.0	0.0	60.7	99.9
1.0000	35.4	15.9	6.1	2.2	0.7	0.2	0.1	0.0	0.0	60.6	99.9
1.0625	35.2	15.8	6.1	2.2	0.7	0.2	0.1	0.0	0.0	60.4	99.9
1.1250	35.0	15.8	6.2	2.2	0.8	0.2	0.1	0.0	0.0	60.2	99.9
1.1875	34.9	15.7	6.2	2.2	0.8	0.3	0.1	0.0	0.0	60.1	99.8
1.2500	34.8	15.7	6.2	2.2	0.8	0.3	0.1	0.0	0.0	60.0	99.8
1.3125	34.7	15.6	6.2	2.3	0.8	0.3	0.1	0.0	0.0	59.9	99.8
1.3750	34.6	15.6	6.2	2.3	0.8	0.3	0.1	0.0	0.0	59.8	99.8
1.4375	34.5	15.6	6.2	2.3	0.8	0.3	0.1	0.0	0.0	59.7	99.7
1.5000	34.5	15.5	6.2	2.3	0.8	0.3	0.1	0.0	0.0	59.7	99.7
1.5625	34.4	15.5	6.2	2.3	0.8	0.3	0.1	0.0	0.0	59.6	99.7
1.6250	34.4	15.5	6.2	2.3	0.8	0.3	0.1	0.0	0.0	59.5	99.7
1.6875	34.3	15.5	6.2	2.3	0.8	0.3	0.1	0.0	0.0	59.5	99.6
1.7500	34.3	15.5	6.2	2.3	0.8	0.3	0.1	0.0	0.0	59.5	99.6
1.8125	34.3	15.5	6.2	2.3	0.8	0.3	0.1	0.0	0.0	59.4	99.6
1.8750	34.3	15.4	6.2	2.3	0.8	0.3	0.1	0.0	0.0	59.4	99.5
1.9375	34.2	15.4	6.2	2.3	0.8	0.3	0.1	0.0	0.0	59.4	99.5
2.0000	34.2	15.4	6.2	2.3	0.8	0.3	0.1	0.0	0.0	59.3	99.5
2.1250	34.2	15.4	6.2	2.3	0.8	0.3	0.1	0.0	0.0	59.3	99.4
2.2500	34.2	15.4	6.2	2.3	0.8	0.3	0.1	0.0	0.0	59.2	99.3
2.3750	34.1	15.4	6.1	2.3	0.8	0.3	0.1	0.0	0.0	59.2	99.3
2.5000	34.1	15.4	6.1	2.3	0.8	0.3	0.1	0.0	0.0	59.2	99.2
2.6250	34.1	15.4	6.1	2.3	0.8	0.3	0.1	0.0	0.0	59.1	99.2
2.7500	34.1	15.3	6.1	2.3	0.8	0.3	0.1	0.0	0.0	59.1	99.1
2.8750	34.0	15.3	6.1	2.3	0.8	0.3	0.1	0.0	0.0	59.1	99.1
3.0000	34.0	15.3	6.1	2.3	0.8	0.3	0.1	0.0	0.0	59.0	99.0
3.2500	34.0	15.3	6.1	2.3	0.8	0.3	0.1	0.0	0.0	58.9	98.9
3.5000	33.9	15.3	6.1	2.3	0.8	0.3	0.1	0.0	0.0	58.9	98.8
3.7500	33.9	15.3	6.1	2.3	0.8	0.3	0.1	0.0	0.0	58.8	98.7
4.0000	33.9	15.3	6.1	2.3	0.8	0.3	0.1	0.0	0.0	58.7	98.6
4.5000	33.8	15.2	6.1	2.3	0.8	0.3	0.1	0.0	0.0	58.6	98.3
5.0000	33.7	15.2	6.1	2.3	0.8	0.3	0.1	0.0	0.0	58.5	98.1
6.0000	33.5	15.1	6.0	2.3	0.8	0.3	0.1	0.0	0.0	58.2	97.6
7.0000	33.4	15.0	6.0	2.3	0.8	0.3	0.1	0.0	0.0	57.9	97.2
8.0000	33.2	15.0	6.0	2.2	0.8	0.3	0.1	0.0	0.0	57.6	96.7
9.0000	33.1	14.9	6.0	2.2	0.8	0.3	0.1	0.0	0.0	57.4	96.3
10.0000	32.9	14.8	5.9	2.2	0.8	0.3	0.1	0.0	0.0	57.1	95.8
11.0000	32.8	14.8	5.9	2.2	0.8	0.3	0.1	0.0	0.0	56.8	95.4
12.0000	32.6	14.7	5.9	2.2	0.8	0.3	0.1	0.0	0.0	56.6	94.9
13.0000	32.5	14.6	5.9	2.2	0.8	0.3	0.1	0.0	0.0	56.3	94.5
14.0000	32.3	14.6	5.8	2.2	0.8	0.3	0.1	0.0	0.0	56.0	94.0
15.0000	32.2	14.5	5.8	2.2	0.8	0.3	0.1	0.0	0.0	55.8	93.6
16.0000	32.0	14.4	5.8	2.2	0.8	0.3	0.1	0.0	0.0	55.5	93.2
17.0000	31.9	14.4	5.7	2.1	0.8	0.3	0.1	0.0	0.0	55.3	92.7
18.0000	31.7	14.3	5.7	2.1	0.8	0.3	0.1	0.0	0.0	55.0	92.3
19.0000	31.6	14.2	5.7	2.1	0.8	0.3	0.1	0.0	0.0	54.7	91.9
20.0000	31.4	14.2	5.7	2.1	0.8	0.3	0.1	0.0	0.0	54.5	91.4

[a]Initial distribution is identical with that in Table 4.1 but the parameters are twice as large: $M = 9$, $a = 1.2000$, $b = 0.6000$, $d = 2.0000$.

Table 4.3. Calculated Behavior of an Open System of Groups According to the LOST Model[a]

Number of groups of each size

Time	1	2	3	4	5	6	7	8	9	Total groups	Total indiv.
0.0000	100.0	0.0	0.0	0.0	0.0	0.0	0.0	0.0	0.0	100.0	100.0
0.0313	94.8	5.0	0.2	0.0	0.0	0.0	0.0	0.0	0.0	100.0	105.3
0.0625	90.5	8.9	0.6	0.0	0.0	0.0	0.0	0.0	0.0	100.0	110.2
0.0938	86.8	11.9	1.2	0.1	0.0	0.0	0.0	0.0	0.0	100.0	114.5
0.1250	83.7	14.3	1.8	0.2	0.0	0.0	0.0	0.0	0.0	100.0	118.5
0.1563	81.0	16.3	2.4	0.3	0.0	0.0	0.0	0.0	0.0	100.0	122.1
0.1875	78.6	17.9	3.0	0.4	0.1	0.0	0.0	0.0	0.0	100.0	125.5
0.2188	76.6	19.1	3.6	0.6	0.1	0.0	0.0	0.0	0.0	100.0	128.5
0.2500	74.8	20.2	4.1	0.7	0.1	0.0	0.0	0.0	0.0	100.0	131.3
0.2813	73.2	21.0	4.7	0.9	0.2	0.0	0.0	0.0	0.0	100.0	133.9
0.3125	71.8	21.8	5.1	1.1	0.2	0.0	0.0	0.0	0.0	100.0	136.2
0.3438	70.6	22.4	5.6	1.2	0.2	0.0	0.0	0.0	0.0	100.0	138.4
0.3750	69.4	22.9	6.0	1.4	0.3	0.1	0.0	0.0	0.0	100.0	140.4
0.4063	68.5	23.3	6.3	1.5	0.3	0.1	0.0	0.0	0.0	100.0	142.3
0.4375	67.6	23.6	6.7	1.7	0.4	0.1	0.0	0.0	0.0	100.0	144.1
0.4688	66.8	23.9	7.0	1.8	0.4	0.1	0.0	0.0	0.0	100.0	145.7
0.5000	66.0	24.2	7.2	1.9	0.5	0.1	0.0	0.0	0.0	100.0	147.2
0.5313	65.4	24.4	7.5	2.1	0.5	0.1	0.0	0.0	0.0	100.0	148.5
0.5625	64.8	24.6	7.7	2.2	0.6	0.1	0.0	0.0	0.0	100.0	149.8
0.5938	64.2	24.7	7.9	2.3	0.6	0.2	0.0	0.0	0.0	100.0	151.0
0.6250	63.7	24.9	8.1	2.4	0.7	0.2	0.0	0.0	0.0	100.0	152.1
0.6563	63.3	25.0	8.3	2.5	0.7	0.2	0.0	0.0	0.0	100.0	153.2
0.6875	62.9	25.1	8.4	2.6	0.7	0.2	0.1	0.0	0.0	100.0	154.1
0.7188	62.5	25.2	8.6	2.7	0.8	0.2	0.1	0.0	0.0	100.0	155.0
0.7500	62.1	25.3	8.7	2.7	0.8	0.2	0.1	0.0	0.0	100.0	155.9
0.7813	61.8	25.3	8.8	2.8	0.8	0.2	0.1	0.0	0.0	100.0	156.6
0.8125	61.5	25.4	9.0	2.9	0.9	0.3	0.1	0.0	0.0	100.0	157.4
0.8438	61.2	25.5	9.1	3.0	0.9	0.3	0.1	0.0	0.0	100.0	158.0
0.8750	61.0	25.5	9.2	3.0	0.9	0.3	0.1	0.0	0.0	100.0	158.7
0.9063	60.8	25.6	9.2	3.1	1.0	0.3	0.1	0.0	0.0	100.0	159.3
0.9375	60.5	25.6	9.3	3.1	1.0	0.3	0.1	0.0	0.0	100.0	159.8
0.9688	60.3	25.6	9.4	3.2	1.0	0.3	0.1	0.0	0.0	100.0	160.3
1.0000	60.2	25.7	9.5	3.2	1.0	0.3	0.1	0.0	0.0	100.0	160.8
1.0625	59.8	25.7	9.6	3.3	1.1	0.3	0.1	0.0	0.0	100.0	161.7
1.1250	59.5	25.7	9.7	3.4	1.1	0.4	0.1	0.0	0.0	100.0	162.4
1.1875	59.3	25.8	9.8	3.4	1.1	0.4	0.1	0.0	0.0	100.0	163.1
1.2500	59.1	25.8	9.9	3.5	1.2	0.4	0.1	0.0	0.0	100.0	163.6
1.3125	58.9	25.8	9.9	3.5	1.2	0.4	0.1	0.0	0.0	100.0	164.1
1.3750	58.7	25.8	10.0	3.6	1.2	0.4	0.1	0.0	0.0	100.0	164.6
1.4375	58.6	25.9	10.0	3.6	1.2	0.4	0.1	0.0	0.0	100.0	164.9
1.5000	58.5	25.9	10.1	3.7	1.3	0.4	0.1	0.0	0.0	100.0	165.3
1.5625	58.4	25.9	10.1	3.7	1.3	0.4	0.1	0.0	0.0	100.0	165.6
1.6250	58.3	25.9	10.1	3.7	1.3	0.4	0.1	0.0	0.0	100.0	165.8
1.6875	58.2	25.9	10.2	3.7	1.3	0.4	0.1	0.0	0.0	99.9	166.0
1.7500	58.1	25.9	10.2	3.7	1.3	0.4	0.1	0.0	0.0	99.9	166.2
1.8125	58.1	25.9	10.2	3.8	1.3	0.4	0.1	0.0	0.0	99.9	166.4
1.8750	58.0	25.9	10.2	3.8	1.3	0.5	0.1	0.0	0.0	99.9	166.5
1.9375	58.0	25.9	10.3	3.8	1.3	0.5	0.1	0.0	0.0	99.9	166.6
2.0000	57.9	25.9	10.3	3.8	1.3	0.5	0.2	0.0	0.0	99.9	166.8
2.1250	57.9	25.9	10.3	3.8	1.4	0.5	0.2	0.0	0.0	99.9	166.9
2.2500	57.8	25.9	10.3	3.8	1.4	0.5	0.2	0.0	0.0	99.9	167.1
2.3750	57.8	25.9	10.3	3.8	1.4	0.5	0.2	0.0	0.0	99.9	167.2
2.5000	57.7	25.9	10.3	3.8	1.4	0.5	0.2	0.0	0.0	99.9	167.2
2.6250	57.7	25.9	10.3	3.9	1.4	0.5	0.2	0.0	0.0	99.9	167.3
2.7500	57.7	25.9	10.3	3.9	1.4	0.5	0.2	0.0	0.0	99.9	167.3
2.8750	57.7	25.9	10.3	3.9	1.4	0.5	0.2	0.0	0.0	99.9	167.3
3.0000	57.7	25.9	10.3	3.9	1.4	0.5	0.2	0.0	0.0	99.8	167.3
3.2500	57.6	25.9	10.3	3.9	1.4	0.5	0.2	0.0	0.0	99.8	167.3
3.5000	57.6	25.9	10.3	3.9	1.4	0.5	0.2	0.0	0.0	99.8	167.3
3.7500	57.6	25.9	10.3	3.9	1.4	0.5	0.2	0.0	0.0	99.8	167.3
4.0000	57.6	25.9	10.3	3.9	1.4	0.5	0.2	0.0	0.0	99.8	167.3
4.5000	57.6	25.9	10.3	.9	1.4	0.5	0.2	0.0	0.0	99.7	167.2
5.0000	57.5	25.9	10.3	3.9	1.4	0.5	0.2	0.0	0.0	99.7	167.2
6.0000	57.5	25.9	10.3	3.9	1.4	0.5	0.2	0.0	0.0	99.6	167.0
7.0000	57.4	25.8	10.3	3.9	1.4	0.5	0.2	0.0	0.0	99.5	166.9
8.0000	57.4	25.8	10.3	3.9	1.4	0.5	0.2	0.0	0.0	99.5	166.8
9.0000	57.3	25.8	10.3	3.9	1.4	0.5	0.2	0.0	0.0	99.4	166.6
10.0000	57.3	25.8	10.3	3.9	1.4	0.5	0.2	0.0	0.0	99.3	166.5
11.0000	57.3	25.8	10.3	3.8	1.4	0.5	0.2	0.0	0.0	99.2	166.4
12.0000	57.2	25.7	10.3	3.8	1.4	0.5	0.2	0.0	0.0	99.1	166.3
13.0000	57.2	25.7	10.3	3.8	1.4	0.5	0.2	0.0	0.0	99.1	166.1
14.0000	57.1	25.7	10.3	3.8	1.4	0.5	0.2	0.0	0.0	99.0	166.0
15.0000	57.1	25.7	10.3	3.8	1.4	0.5	0.2	0.0	0.0	98.9	165.9
16.0000	57.0	25.7	10.3	3.8	1.4	0.5	0.2	0.0	0.0	98.8	165.7
17.0000	57.0	25.6	10.2	3.8	1.4	0.5	0.2	0.0	0.0	98.8	165.6
18.0000	56.9	25.6	10.2	3.8	1.4	0.5	0.2	0.0	0.0	98.7	165.5
19.0000	56.9	25.6	10.2	3.8	1.4	0.5	0.2	0.0	0.0	98.6	165.3
20.0000	56.9	25.6	10.2	3.8	1.4	0.5	0.2	0.0	0.0	98.5	165.2

[a]Initial distribution and parameters are identical with those of Table 4.2: $M = 9$, $a = 1.2000$, $b = 0.6000$, $d = 2.0000$.

Table 4.4. Calculated Behavior of an Open System of Groups According to the LOST Model[a]

	Number of groups of each size										
Time	1	2	3	4	5	6	7	8	9	Total groups	Total indiv.
0.0000	0.0	0.0	0.0	0.0	0.0	0.0	0.0	0.0	100.0	100.0	900.0
0.0313	0.0	0.0	0.0	0.0	0.1	1.1	7.2	28.1	48.9	85.4	722.3
0.0625	0.0	0.0	0.0	0.1	1.0	4.8	15.5	29.9	26.6	77.9	621.2
0.0938	0.0	0.0	0.1	0.6	2.8	9.2	19.6	25.4	15.9	73.6	555.8
0.1250	0.0	0.0	0.3	1.5	5.3	12.8	20.4	20.3	10.3	71.0	508.8
0.1563	0.0	0.1	0.7	2.8	7.9	15.0	19.5	16.1	7.1	69.2	472.2
0.1875	0.0	0.3	1.3	4.4	10.1	16.1	17.7	12.8	5.2	68.0	442.3
0.2188	0.1	0.5	2.2	6.1	11.9	16.3	15.7	10.2	3.9	67.0	416.8
0.2500	0.2	0.9	3.2	7.8	13.2	16.0	13.8	8.3	3.0	66.3	394.6
0.2813	0.3	1.4	4.4	9.3	14.0	15.2	12.1	6.8	2.4	65.8	374.8
0.3125	0.5	2.0	5.6	10.6	14.3	14.3	10.5	5.6	1.9	65.4	356.9
0.3438	0.7	2.7	6.8	11.6	14.4	13.2	9.2	4.7	1.5	65.0	340.6
0.3750	1.1	3.5	8.0	12.4	14.2	12.2	8.1	4.0	1.3	64.7	325.6
0.4063	1.5	4.4	9.1	13.0	13.8	11.2	7.1	3.4	1.1	64.5	311.8
0.4375	2.0	5.3	10.0	13.3	13.3	10.3	6.2	2.9	0.9	64.3	298.9
0.4688	2.6	6.3	10.9	13.5	12.7	9.4	5.5	2.5	0.8	64.1	287.0
0.5000	3.3	7.2	11.6	13.5	12.1	8.6	4.9	2.2	0.7	64.0	275.8
0.5313	4.0	8.1	12.2	13.4	11.4	7.8	4.3	1.9	0.6	63.8	265.3
0.5625	4.9	9.0	12.7	13.2	10.8	7.1	3.9	1.7	0.5	63.7	255.5
0.5938	5.7	9.8	13.0	13.0	10.2	6.5	3.5	1.5	0.4	63.6	246.3
0.6250	6.7	10.6	13.3	12.7	9.6	6.0	3.1	1.3	0.4	63.5	237.6
0.6563	7.6	11.3	13.5	12.3	9.0	5.5	2.8	1.2	0.3	63.5	229.5
0.6875	8.6	12.0	13.6	11.9	8.5	5.0	2.5	1.0	0.3	63.4	221.9
0.7188	9.6	12.6	13.6	11.5	7.9	4.6	2.3	0.9	0.3	63.3	214.7
0.7500	10.7	13.1	13.6	11.1	7.5	4.3	2.1	0.8	0.2	63.3	207.9
0.7813	11.7	13.6	13.5	10.7	7.0	3.9	1.9	0.7	0.2	63.2	201.6
0.8125	12.8	14.1	13.4	10.3	6.6	3.6	1.7	0.7	0.2	63.2	195.6
0.8438	13.8	14.4	13.2	9.9	6.2	3.3	1.6	0.6	0.2	63.2	190.0
0.8750	14.8	14.8	13.0	9.5	5.8	3.1	1.4	0.6	0.2	63.1	184.8
0.9063	15.8	15.1	12.8	9.1	5.5	2.9	1.3	0.5	0.1	63.1	179.8
0.9375	16.8	15.3	12.6	8.7	5.2	2.7	1.2	0.5	0.1	63.1	175.2
0.9688	17.8	15.6	12.4	8.3	4.9	2.5	1.1	0.4	0.1	63.1	170.8
1.0000	18.7	15.8	12.2	8.0	4.6	2.3	1.0	0.4	0.1	63.0	166.7
1.0625	20.5	16.1	11.7	7.4	4.1	2.0	0.9	0.3	0.1	63.0	159.2
1.1250	22.1	16.3	11.2	6.8	3.7	1.8	0.8	0.3	0.1	63.0	152.6
1.1875	23.6	16.4	10.8	6.3	3.3	1.6	0.7	0.2	0.1	62.9	146.8
1.2500	25.0	16.5	10.3	5.8	3.0	1.4	0.6	0.2	0.1	62.9	141.7
1.3125	26.3	16.6	9.9	5.4	2.7	1.2	0.5	0.2	0.0	62.9	137.2
1.3750	27.4	16.6	9.6	5.1	2.5	1.1	0.4	0.2	0.0	62.9	133.3
1.4375	28.4	16.6	9.2	4.7	2.3	1.0	0.4	0.1	0.0	62.8	129.8
1.5000	29.3	16.6	8.9	4.5	2.1	0.9	0.4	0.1	0.0	62.8	126.8
1.5625	30.1	16.6	8.6	4.2	1.9	0.8	0.3	0.1	0.0	62.8	124.1
1.6250	30.9	16.6	8.4	4.0	1.8	0.8	0.3	0.1	0.0	62.8	121.7
1.6875	31.5	16.6	8.2	3.8	1.7	0.7	0.3	0.1	0.0	62.8	119.7
1.7500	32.1	16.6	8.0	3.6	1.6	0.6	0.2	0.1	0.0	62.8	117.9
1.8125	32.6	16.5	7.8	3.5	1.5	0.6	0.2	0.1	0.0	62.8	116.3
1.8750	33.0	16.5	7.6	3.4	1.4	0.6	0.2	0.1	0.0	62.8	114.9
1.9375	33.4	16.5	7.5	3.2	1.3	0.5	0.2	0.1	0.0	62.8	113.7
2.0000	33.7	16.5	7.4	3.1	1.3	0.5	0.2	0.1	0.0	62.8	112.6
2.1250	34.3	16.4	7.2	3.0	1.2	0.4	0.2	0.1	0.0	62.7	110.9
2.2500	34.7	16.4	7.0	2.8	1.1	0.4	0.1	0.0	0.0	62.7	109.5
2.3750	35.1	16.4	6.9	2.8	1.1	0.4	0.1	0.0	0.0	62.7	108.5
2.5000	35.3	16.3	6.8	2.7	1.0	0.4	0.1	0.0	0.0	62.7	107.7
2.6250	35.5	16.3	6.7	2.6	1.0	0.4	0.1	0.0	0.0	62.7	107.1
2.7500	35.7	16.3	6.7	2.6	1.0	0.3	0.1	0.0	0.0	62.7	106.6
2.8750	35.8	16.3	6.6	2.5	0.9	0.3	0.1	0.0	0.0	62.7	106.3
3.0000	35.9	16.3	6.6	2.5	0.9	0.3	0.1	0.0	0.0	62.7	106.0
3.2500	36.0	16.3	6.6	2.5	0.9	0.3	0.1	0.0	0.0	62.7	105.6
3.5000	36.1	16.3	6.5	2.5	0.9	0.3	0.1	0.0	0.0	62.7	105.4
3.7500	36.1	16.3	6.5	2.4	0.9	0.3	0.1	0.0	0.0	62.6	105.2
4.0000	36.1	16.3	6.5	2.4	0.9	0.3	0.1	0.0	0.0	62.6	105.1
4.5000	36.1	16.3	6.5	2.4	0.9	0.3	0.1	0.0	0.0	62.6	105.0
5.0000	36.1	16.2	6.5	2.4	0.9	0.3	0.1	0.0	0.0	62.6	105.0
6.0000	36.1	16.2	6.5	2.4	0.9	0.3	0.1	0.0	0.0	62.5	104.9
7.0000	36.1	16.2	6.5	2.4	0.9	0.3	0.1	0.0	0.0	62.5	104.8
8.0000	36.0	16.2	6.5	2.4	0.9	0.3	0.1	0.0	0.0	62.4	104.7
9.0000	36.0	16.2	6.5	2.4	0.9	0.3	0.1	0.0	0.0	62.4	104.6
10.0000	36.0	16.2	6.5	2.4	0.9	0.3	0.1	0.0	0.0	62.3	104.5
11.0000	35.9	16.2	6.5	2.4	0.9	0.3	0.1	0.0	0.0	62.3	104.4
12.0000	35.9	16.2	6.5	2.4	0.9	0.3	0.1	0.0	0.0	62.2	104.4
13.0000	35.9	16.1	6.5	2.4	0.9	0.3	0.1	0.0	0.0	62.2	104.3
14.0000	35.9	16.1	6.4	2.4	0.9	0.3	0.1	0.0	0.0	62.1	104.2
15.0000	35.8	16.1	6.4	2.4	0.9	0.3	0.1	0.0	0.0	62.1	104.1
16.0000	35.8	16.1	6.4	2.4	0.9	0.3	0.1	0.0	0.0	62.0	104.0
17.0000	35.8	16.1	6.4	2.4	0.9	0.3	0.1	0.0	0.0	62.0	104.0
18.0000	35.7	16.1	6.4	2.4	0.9	0.3	0.1	0.0	0.0	61.9	103.9
19.0000	35.7	16.1	6.4	2.4	0.9	0.3	0.1	0.0	0.0	61.9	103.8
20.0000	35.7	16.1	6.4	2.4	0.9	0.3	0.1	0.0	0.0	61.8	103.7

[a]Parameters are identical with those of Table 4.3 but initial distribution differs: $M = 9$, $a = 1.2000$, $b = 0.6000$, $d = 2.0000$.

61

In Table 4.1, the system starts off with 100 isolates and no other groups. Mixing takes place fairly rapidly at first; after time $t = 2$, changes are very gradual. Given the parameters specified in Table 4.1, (4.21) becomes $dN(t)/dt = -33n_9(t)$. At first there are no groups of size 9, so $N(t)$ is constant at 100. Even by the end of the calculation there are very few groups of size 9 since, when it is rounded to the nearest 0.1, $n_9(20)$ is still zero. However, the fractional number of such groups is enough to produce some decrement in $N(t)$.

Table 4.2 has the same initial distribution as Table 4.1, but the parameters a, b, and d have been doubled. Comparison of Tables 4.1 and 4.2 shows that the rate of mixing has simply been doubled in the latter, as desired, and that the distribution observed at any time in Table 4.2 ($0 \leq t \leq 10$) may be observed at time $2t$ in Table 4.1. The final distributions of the two tables are very close. Ideally, they should be the same at equilibrium, but the system in Table 4.2 has had more time to be affected by the truncation of groups of size 10 and larger.

To see that the system in Table 4.2 has come to equilibrium by $t = 20$, the distribution at that time may be taken as data and a truncated negative binomial distribution fitted to it. Table 4.5 shows the result of using the method of Rider (1955). The estimate of a/d is 0.69 (instead of 0.60) and the estimate of b/d is 0.26 (instead of 0.30). The low value of $X^2 = 0.037$, taken strictly as a numeraire and without attaching any probabilistic implications, suggests good agreement between the "data" and the fitted distribution. Table 4.5 also compares the observed distribution at $t = 20$ with the truncated negative binomial distribution calculated from the true parameter values, making no allowance for truncation loss or any cumulative numerical errors in the differential equations routine. Agreement is almost perfect.

Thus, if the measured parameter values are $a = 1.2$, $b = 0.6$, and $d = 2.0$, the system is guaranteed to be in equilibrium after 20 time units if it is behaving according to the mean of the closed LOST model. But it is not necessary to wait that long to expect the system to have a truncated negative binomial distribution under those condi-

Table 4.5. Calculated Distribution of Group Sizes in the Closed System of Table 4.2

Size of group	Calculated frequency ($t = 20$)	Fitted truncated negative binomial	True truncated negative binomial
1	31.4	30.9	31.5
2	14.2	14.6	14.2
3	5.7	5.9	5.7
4	2.1	2.1	2.1
5	⎧ 0.8	⎧ 0.7	⎧ 0.8
6	1.2 ⎨ 0.3	1.1 ⎨ 0.2	1.2 ⎨ 0.3
≥ 7	⎩ 0.1	⎩ 0.1	⎩ 0.1
		$p = 0.743$	$p = 0.7$
		$r = 2.684$	$r = 2$
		$a/d = 0.690$	$a/d = 0.6$
		$b/d = 0.257$	$b/d = 0.3$
		$\chi^2 = 0.037$	$\chi^2 = 0.001$

tions. Table 4.6 shows the results of fitting a truncated negative binomial distribution to the calculated distributions in Table 4.2 at $t = 0.5$ and $t = 1$. In both cases, the fits are excellent. Hence, with these parameter values, it is not necessary to wait more than half a time unit for the

Table 4.6. Calculated Distribution of Group Sizes in the Closed System of Table 4.2 at $t = 0.5$ and $t = 1$

Size of group	Calculated $t = 0.5$	Fitted truncated negative binomial	Calculated $t = 1.0$	Fitted truncated negative binomial
1	40.9	40.7	35.4	35.0
2	16.9	17.1	15.9	16.2
3	5.4	⎧ 5.5	6.1	6.2
4	1.5	⎪ 1.5	2.2	⎧ 2.1
5	0.4	1.9 ⎨ 0.4	0.7	⎪ 0.7
6	0.1	⎩ 0.1	0.2	3.1 ⎨ 0.2
≥ 7			0.1	⎩ 0.0
		$p = 0.877$		$p = 0.776$
		$r = 5.841$		$r = 3.133$
		$a/d = 0.717$		$a/d = 0.702$
		$b/d = 0.123$		$b/d = 0.224$
		$\chi^2 = 0.006$		$\chi^2 = 0.015$

mean of the closed LOST model to have a truncated negative binomial distribution. However, at least if the method of Rider (1955) is used, the parameter values estimated after only half a time unit may be quite far removed from the true values of the system.

The open system described in Table 4.3 has the same parameter values and initial conditions as that of Table 4.2. It may be checked that the system is very close to equilibrium at $t = 20$, whether the parameters are estimated by the method of Rider or are taken at their true values. Substituting the parameter values and initial conditions into (4.23) yields $dN(0)/dt = 180$. As would be expected, the total number of individuals in the system rises sharply, from 100 to nearly 161, in the first unit of time. Thereafter, the number of individuals rises a bit more, then seems to drop slightly. This drop is probably not a numerical artifact, even though, for example, at $t = 9$, when $N(t)$ is dropping, calculation of the right side of (4.23) yields a small positive value, $dN(9)/dt = 0.64$. It is likely that this positive value is the result of using for $n(9)$, $n_M(9)$, $N(9)$, and $n_1(9)$, the printed values in Table 4.3, which have been rounded to the nearest 0.1, instead of more accurate values.

The open system described in Table 4.4 has the same parameter values as that in Table 4.3, but the system starts with 100 groups all of size 9. Here $dN(0)/dt = -4140$ as calculated from (4.23). The number of individuals drops from 900 to nearly 167 within the first unit of time. Even with these peculiar initial conditions, the approach to a condition of apparent equilibrium is rapid. In Table 4.7, a truncated negative binomial distribution is fitted to the system's distribution at $t = 2$; $X^2 = 0.040$ suggests an excellent fit. Table 4.7 also includes the theoretical distribution calculated with the true parameters, assuming there to be the same number of individuals as were found in the system at $t = 2$. The fit is again good, with $X^2 = 0.893$.

This method of numerical solution of the system equations shows how rapidly a system behaving according to the mean of the LOST models may be expected to approach equilibrium, given parameter values. If time units are chosen so that the parameter values are of the order of

Table 4.7. Calculated Distribution of Group Sizes in the Open System of Table 4.4 at $t = 2$

Size of group	Calculated frequency ($t = 2$)	Fitted truncated negative binomial	True truncated negative binomial
1	33.7	33.0	36.2
2	16.5	17.0	16.3
3	7.4	7.6	6.5
4	3.1	3.2	2.4
5	1.3	1.2 ⎫	0.9 ⎫
6	0.5	0.5 ⎬ 2.0	0.3 ⎬ 1.3
7	0.2	0.2	0.1
⩾ 8	0.1	0.1 ⎭	0.0 ⎭
		$p = 0.685$	$p = 0.7$
		$r = 2.270$	$r = 2$
		$a/d = 0.714$	$a/d = 0.6$
		$b/d = 0.315$	$b/d = 0.3$
		$X^2 = 0.040$	$X^2 = 0.893$

those used in the above examples, then apparent equilibrium will be reached in a small number of time units.

Appendix to Chapter 4: Approximating the Variance

To begin to calculate the equilibrium variance of $n_i(t)$, techniques of Bartlett (1960:31–32) are helpful as follows. (Throughout this section there is a notational ambiguity: sometimes d means a parameter of the LOST model, and sometimes d means the differential of the quantity which follows it. Whenever d stands alone or is followed by i, j, k, or a right or left parenthesis, it refers to the parameter; when d is followed by anything else, it refers to the differential.)

A stochastic version of how the n_i change, $i = 2, 3, \ldots$, implicit in (4.1), is

$$dn_i = [a + b(i - 1)]n_{i-1}dt - (a + bi + c + di)n_i dt \\ + [c + d(i + 1)]n_{i+1}dt + dZ_1 - dZ_2 + dZ_3, \quad (A4.1)$$

where the first three terms are the systematic part of change

65

in n_i; dZ_1, dZ_2, dZ_3 are independent Poisson variables with variances $[a + b(i - 1)]n_{i-1}dt$, $(a + bi + c + di)n_i dt$, and $[c + d(i + 1)]n_{i+1}dt$, respectively but each translated to have mean equal to zero. Consequently, the variance of

$$dZ = dZ_1 - dZ_2 + dZ_3 \qquad (A4.2)$$

is the sum of the variances of the dZ_k, $k = 1, 2, 3$.

Since the limiting expected value of n_i is the constant m_i, let

$$n_i(t) = m_i[1 + u_i(t)], \qquad (A4.3)$$

where, since equilibrium is assumed, u_i will be very small compared to 1. Then

$$du_i = (c + di)(1 + u_{i-1})dt - (a + bi + c + di)$$
$$\times (1 + u_i)dt + (a + bi)(1 + u_{i+1})dt + \frac{dZ}{m_i}. \quad (A4.4)$$

From (A4.4), $u_i + du_i$ may be found by adding u_i to both sides. Bartlett's crucial observation is that at equilibrium, $\text{Var}(u_i + du_i)$ must equal $\text{Var}(u_i)$. Hence, by squaring $u_i + du_i$ and taking the expectation and by noting that the contribution of the independent last term on the right of (A4.4) is

$$\text{Var}\left(\frac{dZ}{m_i}\right) = 2(a + bi + c + di)\frac{dt}{m_i} \qquad (A4.5)$$

we arrive at the result

$$\text{Var}(u_i) = E(u_i^2) = \frac{E(u_i u_{i-1})(c + di)}{a + bi + c + di}$$
$$+ \frac{E(u_i u_{i+1})(a + bi)}{a + bi + c + di} + \frac{1}{m_i}. \qquad (A4.6)$$

Up to this point, the calculation has been exact. The problem in going further is to find the covariance $E(u_i u_{i+1})$. Two approximate routes will now be explored. The first is to assume zero asymptotic covariance between u_i and u_{i+1}, to find $\text{Var}(n_i)$, and then to see how $\text{Var}(n_i)$ would be altered by positive or negative covariances. The second approximate route is to find a two-dimensional partial difference equation for $E(u_i u_{i+k})$, approximate that equation by a simpler one-dimensional linear difference equation with variable coefficients, and solve that equation. This second route constitutes a check on the first.

To set out on the first route, we assume no asymptotic covariance between u_i and u_{i+1}. Then

$$\text{Var}(n_i) = m_i^2 \, \text{Var}(u_i) \sim m_i, \quad i = 2, 3, 4, \ldots . \quad \text{(A4.7)}$$

In the model of an open system presented in Section 4.3, this result (A4.7) holds for $i = 1$ as well. For the closed model, however, a similar calculation shows that, after again dropping terms of smaller order and ignoring covariances,

$$\text{Var}(n_1) \sim \frac{(a+c)m + (b+d)M - (a+b+c+d)m_1 + (c+2d)m_2}{4(a+b)} \quad \text{(A4.8)}$$

where m is the expected total number of groups and M is the expected total number of individuals. Thus, generally, $\text{Var}(n_1) \geq m_1$.

If n_i is taken as an observation of the number of groups of size i while the system is presumed to be at equilibrium, then, as a consequence of (A4.7), the quantity $(n_i - m_i)^2/m_i$ is the square of a variable with expectation zero and standard deviation one. Hence, a sum of such terms (independent by the assumption of zero covariances at equilibrium) has approximately the distribution of χ^2. The use of the χ^2 test of goodness of fit is thus appropriate when the open model may be assumed to have reached equilibrium. When the closed model is appropriate, since

$$\frac{(n_1 - m_1)^2}{\text{Var}(n_1)} < \frac{(n_1 - m_1)^2}{m_1}, \quad \text{(A4.9)}$$

the first term ($i = 1$) in the sum of X^2 will be larger than it ought to be. Hence, if a fit to the open model is accepted using the standard expression for X^2, it is certain to be accepted using the correct value for $\text{Var}(n_1)$; some rejected fits may in fact be acceptable at given probability levels.

The same is true if $E(u_i u_{i+1})$ is positive. From (A4.6), positive covariances will increase $\text{Var}(u_i)$, and the true $\text{Var}(n_i)$ will be greater than m_i. Hence, the relation (A4.9) will hold when the subscripts take other values of i as well. Thus, fits acceptable using the standard expression for X^2

67

are certain to be acceptable using the correct expressions for the variances; some rejected fits may in fact be acceptable at given probability levels. On the other hand, if the covariances are negative, then the standard expression for X^2 may give an acceptably small number, while the true sum of squares of standardized (zero mean, unit variance) variables would be substantially larger.

The second route provides an approximate, but soluble, difference equation for the covariances. Henceforth, it is convenient to take $c = 0$. For $i \neq j$,

$$E(u_i u_j) = E[(u_i + du_i)(u_j + du_j)]$$
$$= E(u_i u_j) + E(u_i du_j) + E(u_j du_i) + 0(u_i^2); \tag{A4.10}$$

hence

$$E(u_i du_j) + E(u_j du_i) = 0. \tag{A4.11}$$

If we use (A4.4) for du_i and du_j in (A4.11) and divide through by dt, and note that $E(dZ/dt) = 0$, then, since there is no covariance between the dZ corresponding to i and the dZ corresponding to j,

$$[2a + (b + d)(i + j)]E(u_i u_j) = diE(u_j u_{i-1})$$
$$+ (a + bi)E(u_j u_{i+1}) + djE(u_i u_{j-1}) \tag{A4.12}$$
$$+ (a + bj)E(u_i u_{j+1}).$$

If we now set $j = i + k$, where $k \geq 1$ and $f(i,k) = E(u_i u_{i+k})$,

$$[2a + 2(b + d)i + (b + d)k]f(i,k) = dif(i - 1, k + 1)$$
$$+ (a + bi)f(i + 1, k - 1) + (di + dk)f(i, k - 1) \tag{A4.13}$$
$$+ (a + bi + bk)f(i, k + 1)$$

for $i \geq 2$ and $k \geq 1$. The restriction on i may be relaxed to $i \geq 1$ for the open model. The boundary conditions for $k = 0$ on (A4.13) follow from (A4.6). For the open model, (A4.6) also gives the boundary condition when $i = 1$, since $u_{i-1} = u_0 = 0$.

On the basis of the analogous one-dimensional second-order difference equation, in which the coefficients vary linearly in the arguments (called the hypergeometric equation by Batchelder 1927), a likely form for the solution of (A4.13) is

$$z(x,y) = \alpha^x x^\beta \gamma^y y^\delta$$

$$\times \left[1 + \frac{s_{10}}{x} + \frac{s_{01}}{y} + \frac{s_{11}}{xy} + \frac{s_{20}}{x^2} + \frac{s_{02}}{y^2} + \cdots \right]. \quad (A4.14)$$

In theory, it is possible, by substituting this form into (A4.13), to evaluate the coefficients α, β, γ, δ, and s. The actual attempt yields an intractable mess, and some simplification seems necessary.

The trivial solutions of (A4.13) are $f(i, k) = 0$ and $f(i, k) = 1$. The first corresponds to the assumption of no covariance explored above, and it is reassuring to see that such an assumption is consistent with the rest of the model. The second implies that the numbers of groups of each size are all locked together deterministically, and it is clearly not the case of interest.

As an approximation to (A4.13), assume there exist values of k large enough so that $f(i, k) \approx f(i, k \pm 1)$; for k in that range define $f(i, k) = g(i)$. By this definition, $g(i)$ is the covariance of the number of groups of size i with the number of groups of size k greater than i when that covariance changes negligibly if k is increased or decreased by 1. Then from (A4.13), in the form of the hypergeometric difference equation studied extensively by Batchelder (1927:68ff), we have

$$(bi + a + b)g(i + 2) - [(b + d)i + (a + b + d)]$$
$$\times g(i + 1) + (di + d)g(i) = 0. \quad (A4.15)$$

Aside from the solutions $g(i) = 0$ and $g(i) = 1$, this equation has the solution

$$g(i) = \left(\frac{d}{b} \right)^{i+1} (i + 1)^{-a/b}$$

$$\times \left[1 + \frac{a}{b(i + 1)} \left(\frac{d}{d - b} - \frac{a}{2b} + \frac{1}{2} \right) + \frac{s_2}{(i + 1)^2} + \cdots \right], \quad (A4.16)$$

where s_2 and further coefficients of the series are still undetermined.

Because of the coefficients in (A4.15), series (A4.16) is divergent (Batchelder 1927:104). While a convergent series that satisfies (A4.15) may be written down (Batchelder 1927:104), that series is not of interest here because it lies in the complex plane off the real line.

Even if the term $s_2/(i + 1)^2$ and all those to the right in (A4.16) are lopped off, the following numerical calculations show that the solution (A4.16) is not the one desired. Table A4.1 gives numerical values of this truncated form of $g(i)$ in (A4.16) for five sets of values of a, b, and d. These five sets of values are estimates derived from observations of nursery school play (Chapter 5). As i increases, this approximate $g(i)$ rapidly approaches infinity, either positive or negative. En route to infinity, $g(i)$ may or may not change signs. For small i, $g(i)$ may be positive or negative. This information only adds to the confusion.

Since the covariance of two variables each small with respect to 1 cannot approach infinity, I reject (A4.16) as the solution of interest. As before, the solution $g(i) = 1$ corresponds to having all of the numbers of groups of each size change in lockstep, so the only remaining solution is $g(i) = 0$. The failure to find a satisfactory nonzero expression for the covariances may be because, in fact, there is none or because the transition from the exact equation (A4.13) to an approximation (A4.15) eliminates that solution.

The best that can be said at the moment is that approximating the covariances by zero is consistent with the model and that no better nonzero approximation can be had. As a result, and pending a better treatment of the problem, the use of the χ^2 test to measure goodness of fit seems acceptable.

Table A4.1. Value of $g(i)$ for Selected Parameter Values[a]

| Date | Parameter values | | | Values of $g(i)$ | | | | | |
	a	b	d	$i = 1$	$i = 2$	$i = 3$	$i = 4$	$i = 5$	$i = 6$
1.27	.093	.018	.173	−3.85	−2.03	−1.65	.01	12.57	93.24
1.28	.051	.026	.201	25.40	76.94	312.58	1482.90	—	—
1.29	0	.065	.369	32.23	182.95	1038.61	—	—	—
2.7	.081	.010	.149	−7.31	−2.57	−2.63	−4.82	−12.77	−43.48
2.141	.080	.020	.168	1.19	3.76	12.35	47.38	205.13	—

[a]Dashes indicate values not calculated. Dates and parameter values originate from Table 5.11.

5
Nursery
School
Play:
LOST
Dynamics
Found

5.1 Cambridge Nursery School

To test in detail the dynamics assumed by the linear one-step transition (LOST) models I observed the free play of four-year-olds in the Cambridge Nursery School. The children, apparently middle class, arrived at school between 9:00 and 9:15 A.M. and had a period of free play extending usually until 10:30. Group activities, such as listening to stories or singing, as well as necessarily isolating activities, such as resting or drinking juice, were scheduled for later in the morning. Toys, tables, easels, and play equipment were available throughout the room, which had inside dimensions of 21 feet by 21 feet 6 inches. No interactive groupings were imposed by the geometry of the room, though often children not in apparent interaction would work around the same large play table. There were two doors to the playroom, one leading to the bathroom and the second, to another playroom for three-year-olds. The children were allowed to enter and leave as they liked (making this an open system with a variable number of groups). While excursions were frequently necessary to borrow play equipment from or to return it to the other room, long exchanges between the three- and four-year-olds were discouraged.

Under these circumstances, the children's play groups seemed to fit exactly James's definition (1953:569) of "freely forming" groups as "those whose members are relatively free to maintain or break off contact with one another, that is, they are ones where informal controls on behavior are at work and spontaneity is at a maximum."

To make my observations, I sat quietly in one corner of the room with stopwatch and notebook in full sight of the children, starting between 9:15 and 9:30. The first day of observation was devoted to trying various recording techniques and to accustoming the children and me to each other. After I had been sitting in the corner for half an hour without introduction and completely ignored by the teacher, one child pointed out to her that there was a man sitting in the corner. She answered that I was there to learn about children. Thereafter the children genuinely seemed to ignore me, to an extent that surprised even the teacher. They did not hesitate to use the table in my corner or to get toys on the shelves near me, but they also did not congregate around me or try to play with me. I therefore feel fairly confident that more sophisticated apparatus like a one-way observing mirror would not have altered the results.

Associations of children which I counted as groups were as nearly as possible those which met the criteria of James (1951:475) given in Section 1.2, namely, "groups in which the members were in face-to-face interaction as evidenced by the criteria of gesticulation, laughter, smiles, talk, play or work. Individuals who merely occupied contiguous space were not counted as members of a group." Whereas James had a pair of observers acting as counter and recorder, my observations were made alone.

On the basis of the trial day of observation, I chose to record the state of the system of groups in the playroom at 30-second intervals. This interval allowed me enough time to record my observations with a reasonably small chance of error, and it seemed short enough at the usual tempo of play so that more than one departure from or more than one arrival to any given group was rare. The adequacy of this interval for excluding "simultaneous" events (two or more arrivals or departures in a given group) will be checked against the data in Section 5.4. The procedure was simply to sweep the room visually and write down the size of each group. The two adults usually in the room (the teacher and her helper) were ignored, so that a child grouped with one of them counted as an isolate. The adults spent most of their time walking around providing or picking up toys; nearly all of the children's interactions were with each other.

Since only the size of each group was recorded, information about individual differences, such as is available from Struhsaker's data, was lost. The simple technology for making observations did not permit recording the individual composition of groups and was inadequate for recording just group sizes during the free play of three-year-olds, whose tempo of play and social exchange was much faster. The three-year-olds probably would have required intervals not longer than 15 seconds. A more serious implication for testing LOST dynamics of this way of recording the state of the system will be presented in Section 5.4. The data appear in Tables 5.1–5.7. The first column lists the number of the epoch of observation, starting from 1. The second column lists the number of groups in the system at each epoch, and the third lists the number of individuals. Each single-digit number in the fourth column is the size of a group. Thus, the array "2111111" (the first observation on 27 January 1969) specifies that 1 pair and 6 isolates were observed, giving a total of 7 groups and 8 individuals. For convenience of reference, each day's set of data was given a code number corresponding to the date (1.27 for 27 January). Observations were made during six mornings. On the last of these (Valentine's Day, 14 February), the teacher read a story to some of the children during the usual free play period. The data counting those children who sat listening to the teacher as a group appear as set 2.141, while the same morning's observations excluding such nonfreely forming groups appear as set 2.142.

5.2 Parting with Partitions

In Section 3.2, the model of the random partitioning of indistinguishable individuals into indistinguishable groups was fairly successful in describing Struhsaker's data. The dismissal there of an almost zero-parameter model on qualitative grounds may have left a lingering suspicion that the model was not quantitatively bad. The present nursery school data dispel that suspicion.

From the 6 sets of data on freely forming groups (excluding set 2.141 with the story groups), the epochs were sorted by the number of individuals in the system. For 70 of the epochs observed, the system had 7 individuals; for 55

Table 5.1. Observations of Group Sizes During Free Play at Cambridge Nursery School, 27 January 1969 (Set 1.27)[a]

Epoch	Groups	Individuals	Sizes of groups	Epoch	Groups	Individuals	Sizes of groups
1	7	8	2111111	46	9	9	111111111
2	6	8	311111	47	7	9	2211111
3	7	8	2111111	48	6	9	321111
4	8	8	11111111	49	6	9	411111
5	8	9	21111111	50	7	9	3111111
6	8	9	21111111	51	7	9	2211111
7	7	9	2211111	52	7	10	3211111
8	7	8	2111111	53	9	11	221111111
9	6	8	221111	54	10	11	2111111111
10	5	7	31111	55	9	11	311111111
11	5	6	21111	56	10	11	2111111111
12	5	6	21111	57	9	10	211111111
13	5	6	21111	58	8	11	32111111
14	6	6	111111	59	9	11	221111111
15	5	6	21111	60	8	11	22211111
16	6	7	211111	61	10	11	2111111111
17	5	7	22111	< 62	8	10	22111111
18	4	7	3211	63	6	9	411111
19	3	7	331	64	7	10	4111111
20	5	7	22111	65	7	10	3211111
21	6	6	111111	66	8	10	22111111
22	5	6	21111	67	6	10	322111
23	6	7	211111	68	6	10	421111
24	7	8	2111111	69	6	10	421111
25	5	8	32111	70	7	10	3211111
26	7	8	2111111	71	8	10	31111111
27	6	8	311111	72	8	10	22111111
28	6	8	311111	73	6	10	222211
29	5	9	32211	74	7	9	2211111
30	6	9	321111	75	7	9	2211111
31	9	10	211111111	76	6	9	321111
32	7	10	3211111	77	4	9	4221
33	9	10	211111111	78	4	9	3321
34	10	10	1111111111	79	6	9	222111
35	8	10	22111111	80	4	9	3321
36	7	9	2211111	81	5	9	32211
< 37	8	8	11111111	82	7	9	2211111
38	6	8	311111	83	7	9	2211111
39	7	8	2111111	84	7	9	2211111
40	7	8	2111111	85	7	9	2211111
41	4	8	3221	86	5	9	32211
42	7	8	2111111	87	7	9	2211111
43	6	7	211111	< 88	8	9	21111111
< 44	6	8	311111	89	6	9	411111
45	9	9	111111111				

[a]Bracket (<) between two epochs in Tables 5.1 - 5.7 indicates multiple arrivals to or departures from some group.

75

Table 5.2. Observations of Group Sizes During Free Play at Cambridge Nursery School, 28 January 1969 (set 1.28)

Epoch	Groups	Indi-viduals	Sizes of groups		Epoch	Groups	Indi-viduals	Sizes of groups
1	9	9	111111111		52	6	6	111111
2	7	9	2211111		53	7	7	1111111
3	8	9	21111111		54	6	7	211111
4	8	9	21111111		55	5	7	31111
5	8	9	21111111		56	5	7	31111
6	8	9	21111111		57	4	7	4111
7	8	10	22111111		58	5	7	31111
8	9	9	111111111		59	6	7	211111
9	9	9	111111111		60	5	7	22111
10	9	9	111111111		61	6	7	211111
11	8	9	21111111		62	6	7	211111
12	7	9	3111111		63	4	7	2221
13	8	9	21111111		64	5	7	22111
14	8	9	21111111		65	5	7	22111
15	7	9	2211111		66	4	7	3211
16	8	8	11111111		67	5	7	22111
17	8	8	11111111		68	7	8	2111111
18	6	7	211111		69	7	8	2111111
19	6	7	211111		70	6	8	221111
20	6	7	211111		71	6	8	311111
21	6	7	211111	< 72	4	8	4211
22	5	7	22111	73	6	7	211111
23	4	7	3211		74	7	8	2111111
24	4	7	3211		75	8	9	21111111
25	5	7	31111		76	9	9	111111111
26	4	7	2221		77	8	9	21111111
27	5	7	31111		78	7	9	2211111
28	6	8	311111		79	7	9	2211111
29	6	8	221111		80	7	9	2211111
30	4	8	3221		81	7	9	2211111
31	6	8	221111		82	8	9	21111111
32	4	8	3311		83	5	9	32211
33	4	8	3221		84	7	9	2211111
34	5	8	32111		85	6	9	321111
35	7	8	2111111		86	6	9	321111
36	7	8	2111111		87	6	9	411111
37	6	7	211111		88	5	9	42111
38	6	7	211111		89	6	9	321111
39	7	7	1111111		90	5	9	33111
40	6	7	211111		91	6	9	321111
41	6	7	211111		92	7	8	2111111
42	6	7	211111		93	8	9	21111111
43	6	7	211111		94	7	9	2211111
44	5	7	22111		95	7	9	3111111
45	6	7	211111		96	7	9	3111111
46	6	7	211111		97	7	9	2211111
47	6	7	211111		98	7	9	2211111
48	7	7	1111111		99	7	9	2211111
49	5	7	22111		100	7	9	2211111
50	5	7	22111		101	5	9	33111
51	6	7	211111					

Table 5.3. Observations of Group Sizes During Free Play at Cambridge Nursery School, 29 January 1969 (Set 1.29)

Epoch	Groups	Individuals	Sizes of groups	Epoch	Groups	Individuals	Sizes of groups
1	9	10	211111111	40	7	9	2211111
2	9	10	211111111	41	8	9	21111111
3	9	10	211111111	42	7	10	3211111
4	7	8	2111111	43	8	10	22111111
5	10	10	1111111111	44	8	9	21111111
6	8	10	22111111	45	8	9	21111111
7	8	10	22111111	46	6	8	311111
8	7	10	3211111	47	7	9	2211111
9	7	10	3211111	< 48	7	10	3211111
10	6	10	322111	49	6	10	511111
11	8	10	22111111	50	6	10	421111
12	7	10	2221111	< 51	6	10	421111
13	8	10	22111111	52	7	10	2221111
14	7	10	3211111	53	7	10	2221111
15	6	10	421111	54	6	10	322111
16	8	11	32111111	55	5	10	32221
17	7	10	3211111	56	6	10	322111
18	7	10	3211111	57	7	10	3211111
19	7	10	2221111	58	7	10	3211111
20	7	10	2221111	59	7	10	3211111
21	8	10	22111111	60	6	10	322111
22	8	10	22111111	61	7	10	2221111
23	8	10	22111111	62	5	9	32211
24	6	9	222111	63	9	10	211111111
25	6	9	222111	64	7	10	3211111
26	7	9	2211111	65	6	10	421111
27	7	9	2211111	66	6	10	322111
28	7	9	2211111	67	6	10	322111
29	6	9	222111	68	8	10	31111111
30	6	9	222111	69	8	10	31111111
31	8	10	22111111	70	6	10	421111
32	7	10	3211111	71	6	10	322111
< 33	6	10	421111	72	6	10	322111
< 34	5	10	61111	73	7	10	4111111
< 35	7	10	2221111	74	6	10	421111
36	7	10	2221111	< 75	6	10	421111
37	9	10	211111111	76	8	10	22111111
38	8	10	31111111	77	7	10	2221111
39	6	8	311111	78	8	10	31111111

Table 5.4. Observations of Group Sizes During Free Play at Cambridge Nursery School, 7 February 1969 (Set 2.7)

Epoch	Groups	Indi-viduals	Sizes of groups	Epoch	Groups	Indi-viduals	Sizes of groups
1	7	7	1111111	49	7	9	2211111
2	6	7	211111	50	6	9	321111
3	5	7	31111	51	9	11	221111111
4	3	6	411	52	8	11	32111111
5	3	6	411	53	7	11	3221111
6	3	6	411	54	8	11	32111111
7	4	6	3111	55	8	11	22211111
8	5	7	31111	56	8	11	32111111
9	5	6	21111	57	6	11	332111
10	5	7	31111	58	7	11	3221111
11	3	6	411	59	7	11	3221111
12	3	5	311	60	9	11	311111111
13	4	6	3111	61	7	10	3211111
14	3	6	321	62	6	10	331111
15	5	8	32111	63	6	10	331111
16	5	8	32111	64	6	10	331111
17	5	8	32111	65	6	10	331111
18	7	9	2211111	66	6	10	331111
19	7	9	2211111	67	6	10	322111
20	6	9	321111	68	5	9	33111
21	6	9	321111	69	5	9	32211
22	5	9	42111	70	6	9	321111
23	5	9	42111	71	7	10	3211111
24	6	10	421111	72	6	10	331111
25	7	10	3211111	73	7	10	3211111
26	7	11	3221111	74	7	10	3211111
27	6	10	322111	75	7	10	3211111
28	7	10	3211111	76	6	9	222111
29	8	10	22111111	77	6	9	222111
30	8	11	22211111	78	5	9	32211
31	7	11	3221111	79	7	10	3211111
32	7	10	3211111	80	6	9	321111
33	8	11	22211111	⟨81	6	10	421111
34	7	11	3221111	⟨82	6	9	222111
35	8	10	22111111	83	8	10	22111111
36	8	10	22111111	84	7	10	3211111
37	8	10	31111111	85	8	10	22111111
⟨38	7	10	4111111	86	7	10	3211111
⟨39	7	10	2221111	⟨87	7	11	3311111
40	7	10	3211111	⟨88	9	10	211111111
41	7	10	2221111	⟨89	7	11	3311111
42	9	10	211111111	90	7	11	3311111
43	9	11	221111111	91	8	11	32111111
44	9	11	221111111	92	8	10	31111111
45	9	11	221111111	93	8	11	32111111
46	8	11	22211111	94	8	11	22211111
47	9	10	211111111	95	8	10	31111111
48	7	9	2211111				

Table 5.5. Observations of Group Sizes During Free Play at Cambridge Nursery School, 12 February 1969 (Set 2.12)

Epoch	Groups	Indi-viduals	Sizes of groups	Epoch	Groups	Indi-viduals	Sizes of groups
1	7	7	1111111	42	7	9	2211111
2	6	7	211111	43	7	9	2211111
3	7	7	1111111	44	6	9	222111
4	6	7	211111	45	8	9	21111111
5	7	7	1111111	46	7	9	2211111
6	6	7	211111	47	6	9	222111
7	7	8	2111111	48	7	9	2211111
8	5	8	32111	49	6	9	321111
9	7	8	2111111	50	6	9	321111
10	6	9	321111	51	5	9	32211
11	8	9	21111111	52	5	9	32211
12	6	9	222111	53	5	9	32211
13	8	9	21111111	54	5	9	32211
14	8	9	21111111	55	5	9	33111
15	8	9	21111111	56	7	9	3111111
16	8	9	21111111	57	7	9	2211111
17	6	9	222111	58	8	9	21111111
18	6	9	321111	59	4	8	3221
19	8	9	21111111	60	5	8	22211
20	5	9	22221	61	6	8	221111
21	7	9	2211111	62	6	9	222111
22	8	9	21111111	63	6	8	221111
23	6	9	222111	64	6	9	321111
24	8	9	21111111	65	7	9	2211111
25	8	9	21111111	66	6	9	222111
26	7	9	2211111	67	6	9	222111
27	7	9	2211111	68	7	9	3111111
28	6	9	321111	69	7	9	3111111
29	7	9	2211111	70	7	9	2211111
30	8	9	21111111	71	6	9	222111
31	8	9	21111111	72	7	9	3111111
32	8	9	21111111	73	6	9	321111
33	8	9	21111111	74	6	9	321111
34	9	9	111111111	75	6	9	321111
35	8	9	21111111	76	4	9	4311
36	7	9	2211111	77	5	8	32111
37	7	9	2211111	78	6	9	321111
38	7	9	2211111	79	5	9	32211
39	6	9	222111	80	6	9	222111
40	7	9	2211111	81	5	9	42111
41	7	9	2211111	82	5	9	42111

Table 5.6. Observations of Group Sizes During Free Play at Cambridge Nursery School, 14 February 1969 (Set 2.142)[a]

Epoch	Groups	Individuals	Sizes of groups	Epoch	Groups	Individuals	Sizes of groups
1	5	7	22111	43	4	7	3211
2	4	7	3211	44	4	7	3211
3	5	7	22111	45	4	5	2111
4	5	7	22111	46	4	5	2111
5	6	7	211111	47	5	5	11111
⎡6	4	7	2221	48	4	5	2111
⎣7	5	8	41111	49	4	5	2111
8	4	8	4211	50	4	6	2211
9	5	9	42111	51	4	6	2211
10	6	9	321111	⎡52	4	6	2211
11	6	9	222111	⎢53	3	6	411
12	7	9	3111111	⎣54	3	5	221
13	8	11	22211111	55	4	8	3311
14	8	11	32111111	56	6	8	221111
15	10	12	2211111111	57	6	7	211111
16	9	12	222111111	58	4	8	3221
17	10	13	3211111111	59	10	13	2221111111
18	12	13	211111111111	60	9	13	322111111
19	9	12	321111111	61	8	13	32221111
20	10	13	2221111111	62	10	13	2221111111
21	13	13	1111111111111	63	8	12	32211111
⎡22	13	13	1111111111111	64	9	13	322111111
⎣23	10	13	3211111111	65	8	12	32211111
24	11	13	31111111111	66	9	12	321111111
25	10	13	2221111111	67	9	12	321111111
26	11	13	22111111111	68	10	12	2211111111
27	10	13	3211111111	69	10	13	2221111111
28	10	13	3211111111	70	11	13	22111111111
29	10	13	3211111111	71	9	12	222111111
30	11	13	22111111111	72	10	13	3211111111
31	10	13	2221111111	73	9	13	331111111
32	9	14	322211111	74	9	13	322111111
33	11	13	22111111111	75	8	13	42211111
34	11	13	22111111111	76	9	13	322111111
⎡35	11	13	22111111111	77	9	13	322111111
⎣36	7	13	4321111	⎡78	8	14	43211111
37	9	13	322111111	⎣79	7	9	2211111
38	10	13	2221111111	80	7	9	2211111
39	10	12	2211111111	81	7	9	2211111
40	7	11	3221111	82	6	9	222111
41	6	11	332111	⎡83	9	9	111111111
42	5	7	22111	⎣84	10	13	3211111111
				85	9	13	222211111

[a]Groups listening to a Valentine's Day story are excluded.

Table 5.7. Observations of Group Sizes During Free Play at Cambridge Nursery School, 14 February 1969 (Set 2.141)[a]

Epoch	Groups	Indi-viduals	Sizes of groups	Epoch	Groups	Indi-viduals	Sizes of groups
1	5	7	22111	43	5	11	43211
2	4	7	3211	< 44	5	11	43211
3	5	7	22111	45	5	11	62111
4	5	7	22111	46	5	11	62111
5	6	7	211111	47	6	11	611111
< 6	4	7	2221	48	5	11	62111
7	5	8	41111	49	5	11	62111
8	4	8	4211	50	5	12	62211
9	5	9	42111	51	5	12	62211
10	6	9	321111	52	5	12	62211
11	6	9	222111	< 53	4	12	6411
12	7	9	3111111	< 54	4	12	7221
13	8	11	22211111	55	5	13	53311
14	8	11	32111111	56	7	13	5221111
15	10	12	2211111111	57	7	13	6211111
16	9	12	222111111	< 58	5	13	53221
17	10	13	3211111111	59	10	13	2221111111
18	12	13	211111111111	60	9	13	322111111
19	9	12	321111111	61	8	13	32221111
20	10	13	2221111111	62	10	13	2221111111
21	13	13	1111111111111	63	8	12	32211111
< 22	13	13	1111111111111	64	9	13	322111111
23	10	13	3211111111	65	8	12	32211111
24	11	13	31111111111	66	9	12	321111111
25	10	13	2221111111	67	9	12	321111111
26	11	13	22111111111	68	10	12	2211111111
27	10	13	3211111111	69	10	13	2221111111
28	10	13	3211111111	70	11	13	22111111111
29	10	13	3211111111	71	9	12	222111111
30	11	13	22111111111	72	10	13	3211111111
31	10	13	2221111111	73	9	13	331111111
32	9	14	322211111	74	9	13	322111111
33	11	13	22111111111	75	8	13	42211111
34	11	13	22111111111	76	9	13	322111111
< 35	11	13	22111111111	77	9	13	322111111
36	7	13	4321111	78	8	14	43211111
37	9	13	322111111	79	8	13	42211111
38	10	13	2221111111	80	8	13	42211111
39	10	12	2211111111	81	8	13	42211111
40	7	11	3221111	82	7	13	4222111
41	6	11	332111	83	10	13	4111111111
42	6	11	422111	84	10	13	3211111111
				85	9	13	222211111

[a]Groups listening to a Valentine's Day story are included.

81

epochs, it had 8; for 177, 9; and for 116, 10. None of the other total numbers of individuals appeared more than 50 times. The frequency distribution of the number of groups per epoch when there were 7, 8, 9, or 10 individuals in the system is given in Table 5.8. Next to each observed frequency distribution are given the frequencies of occurrence of each number of parts (corresponding to number of groups) in the partitions of 7, 8, 9, or 10.

Whereas the frequencies of the numbers of parts of partitions monotonically decrease in the range of observed numbers of groups, the mode of the observed frequency distributions of number of groups is clearly closer to the number of individuals in the system. Even with such crude statistics, it is obvious that the model of random partitioning does not give predictions of the same form as the observations and may be rejected.

5.3 Equilibrium Distributions

As a first check on whether the dynamics of the LOST models apply to nursery school play, the observed overall distributions of group size on each day will be compared with the equilibrium distribution predicted by the LOST models. The overall distribution of group size for each day is obtained from the data in Tables 5.1–5.7 by simply counting the total number of isolates, pairs, and so on in all epochs of that day. The assumption made here that the children's play may be regarded as being at equilibrium, rather than in a transient state approaching equilibrium, will be checked and confirmed in the next section. The validity of using the distribution of size of single groups rather than the distribution of states of the system follows from the linearity of the models (Section 4.1). The validity of using the χ^2 test to measure goodness of fit rests (precariously, for the moment) on the analysis attempted in the Appendix to Chapter 4.

Table 5.9 gives the 7 observed frequency distributions of group size along with fitted truncated negative binomial or truncated Poisson distributions. According to the χ^2 test, the fits may not be rejected at the 0.01 level for 5 of

Table 5.8. Observed Frequency Distributions of Number of Groups in the Nursery School Playroom

| | Number of individuals in system[a] | | | | | | | |
| | 7 | | 8 | | 9 | | 10 | |
Number of groups	Obs. freq.	Freq. in partitions[b]	Obs. freq.	Freq. in partitions	Obs. freq.	Freq. in partitions	Obs. freq.	Freq. in partitions
1	0	1	0	1	0	1	0	1
2	0	3	0	4	0	4	0	5
3	1	4	0	5	0	7	0	8
4	11	3	9	5	4	6	0	9
5	23	2	9	3	23	5	2	7
6	28	1	16	2	48	3	31	5
7	7	1	17	1	60	2	42	3
8	—	—	4	1	33	1	28	2
9	—	—	—	—	9	1	11	1
10	—	—	—	—	—	—	2	1

[a]Only total numbers of individuals observed more than 50 times are included.
[b]Observations are compared with the frequency of number of parts in partitions of the total number of individuals.

Table 5.9 Frequency Distributions of Group Size in Free Play of Four-Year-Olds at Cambridge Nursery School

Set	Group size	Observed frequency	Predicted frequency	Truncated negative binomial	
1.27	1	460	458.6	$p = 0.786$	$x^2 = 1.631$
	2	101	107.8	$r = 1.197$	df = 1
	3	30	24.6	$a = 0.256$	$0.2 < P < 0.3$
	$\geqslant 4$	7	7.1	$b = 0.214$	
1.28	1	498	497.0	$p = 0.855$	$x^2 = 1.569$
	2	106	111.1	$r = 2.076$	df = 1
	3	27	22.0	$a = 0.302$	$0.2 < P < 0.3$
	$\geqslant 4$	4	4.9	$b = 0.145$	
1.29	1	388	388.4	$p = 0.809$	$x^2 = 0.472$
	2	120	118.1	$r = 2.187$	df = 2
	3	29	31.4	$a = 0.417$	$0.7 < P < 0.8$
	4	9	7.8	$b = 0.191$	
	$\geqslant 5$	2	2.4		
2.7	1	436	430.6	$p = 0.790$	$x^2 = 27.039$
	2	112	139.9	$r = 2.094$	df = 1
	3	68	40.1	$a = 0.440$	$P < 0.01$
	$\geqslant 4$	9	14.4	$b = 0.210$	

Set	Group size	Observed frequency	Predicted frequency	Truncated poisson
2.12[a]	1	385	387.9	$\lambda = a = 0.615$
	2	123	119.3	$x^2 = 0.528$
	3	25	24.5	df = 2
	$\geqslant 4$	3	4.3	$0.7 < P < 0.8$
2.142 (without stories)	1	473	466.9	$\lambda = a = 0.648$
	2	140	151.3	$x^2 = 1.637$
	3	37	32.7	df = 2
	$\geqslant 4$	7	6.1	$0.3 < P < 0.5$

Set	Group size	Observed frequency	Predicted frequency	Truncated negative binomial	
2.141 (with stories)	1	473	474.5	$p = 0.508$	$x^2 = 22.567$
	2	140	130.0	$r = 0.115$	df = 4
	3	37	45.1	$a = 0.057$	$P < 0.01$
	4	15	17.3	$b = 0.492$	
	5	3	7.0		
	6	10	2.9		
	$\geqslant 7$	1	2.3		

[a]This set failed the Sampford criterion for the truncated negative binomial.

the 6 sets where they would be expected to be good; the fit to the data including the storytelling groups (set 2.141) must be rejected at the 0.01 level. So, in general, an open LOST model describes the distribution of group sizes.

5.4 Checking the Dynamics

This section obtains estimates of the LOST parameters a, b, and d from the changes over time in the state of the system of play groups; and it shows that, with these parameter values, the system should be expected to be in equilibrium after a very short time. It also compares, by means of a very powerful statistical technique, the jackknife, these dynamic estimates of a/d and b/d with those obtained from fitting the equilibrium distribution. Then, upon finding that the dynamic and equilibrium estimates cannot be distinguished within the variability of the data, we consider how seriously the details of the LOST models can be taken.

From each day's data, frequency distributions of arrivals to or departures from groups of each size were compiled by comparing successive states of the system. An example illustrates the procedure. In the first three epochs on 27 January, the group sizes observed, after sorting in non-increasing order, were as follows:

Epoch	Group sizes
1	2111111
2	311111
3	2111111

The first and second epochs were compared column by column, out to the last column to the right for which both epochs had nonzero group sizes. In the first column of group sizes, the "2" in epoch 1 became a "3" in epoch 2; so in the histogram by group size of arrivals and departures, the number of arrivals to groups of size 2 was increased (from zero initially) by 1. For the next five columns to the right, groups of size 1 remained at size 1, so no further change was made in the histogram of arrivals and departures. Comparing the second and third epochs, one sees a departure from a group of size 3 in the first column with no other changes.

85

In the 6 sets of data excluding storytelling, there were a total of 530 epochs of observation, or 524 transitions from one epoch to the next. Of these 524, 30 (5.7 percent) showed changes in the size of a group by more than one individual. For example, in the first day's data (set 1.27), between epochs 62 and 63 there were two arrivals to a group of size 2, and the same occurred between epochs 88 and 89. In the output (Table B5.4) of a simulation (Appendix B to this chapter) of a LOST process, there were 20 transitions out of 599 which showed changes in the size of a group by more than one individual. Since the simulation is known to be a LOST process, the presence of multiple events in the observations of the nursery school is not grounds for concluding they could not have come from a LOST process. However, the dynamic estimation procedures which follow assume the fiction that within $dt = 30$ seconds no such multiple events occur. While the bias introduced by this counterfactual assumption has not been explored in detail, the magnitude of the bias should be small since multiple events were in fact so rare.

In the data set 2.141 (with storytelling), 8 out of the 84 transitions (9.5 percent) had multiple arrivals or departures, principally because when the story terminated, the large groups listening decomposed into individuals. This sudden transition in size showed that the groups were not being held together by the mutual attraction of the members but by the story.

A multiple arrival (departure) could be counted as arrivals to (departures from) groups changing in size one step at a time or as several arrivals to (departures from) a group fixed in size. For example, the transition from a group of size 2 to a group of size 4 could be recorded either as one arrival to a group of size 2 and another arrival to a group of size 3 or as two arrivals to a group of size 2. Since I assumed that the groups in the system were responding to the state of the system at the beginning of each interval, I preferred the latter form of accounting.

The number of departures from groups of size 1 must be zero, since if a "1" in one epoch is replaced in the following epoch by a zero (a blank), that column is excluded from the counting procedure.

The entire procedure of preparing the histograms by group size of arrivals and departures was mechanized, and the correctness of the computing program was checked against hand computations with samples of data.

This method of recording the state of the system of groups and of inferring transitions just from the sizes of the groups has (at least) one important failing, best illustrated by returning to the observations of the first three epochs of set 1.27 cited above. Although the counting procedure used infers that one individual arrived at a group of size 2 in the transition from the first epoch to the second, it is also possible that the two individuals paired at epoch one split up and that three other individuals isolated at epoch one joined into a triple at epoch two. Similar alternative interpretations are possible for most of the other changes from one epoch to another. Without identification of the individuals in each group at each epoch, it is not possible to prove that these alternative routes of change were not followed, and the technology used for recording and observing was inadequate to identify individuals and still maintain 30-second intervals. I can only say that after paying attention to the individual composition of groups during the trial day of observation, I felt confident that within 30-second intervals, nearly all groups changed by the arrival or departure of single individuals and that representing the state of the system merely by group sizes would not misrepresent the transitions between groups. My confidence is subject to revision by better evidence.

The seven histograms by group size of arrivals and departures are listed in Table 5.10. In the following description of how the LOST parameters, a, b, and d were estimated from this information (separately for each day), the number of arrivals to groups of size i is referred to as A_i and the number of departures from groups of size i as D_i. Also, the total number of groups of size i observed is

$$N_i = \sum_t n_i(t), \qquad (5.1)$$

where $n_i(t)$ is the number of groups of size i observed at each epoch t and the sum is over all epochs of observation

Table 5.10. Frequency Distributions of Arrivals to and Departures From Each Size of Group in Each Day's Observations

Set	Group size	Arrivals	Departures
1.27	1	29	0
	2	23	27
	3	3	22
	4	0	4
	5	0	0
	6	0	0
	7	0	0
1.28	1	29	0
	2	15	27
	3	3	12
	4	0	4
	5	0	0
	6	0	0
	7	0	0
1.29	1	22	0
	2	11	22
	3	7	7
	4	2	7
	5	0	1
	6	0	4
	7	0	0
2.7	1	23	0
	2	20	20
	3	5	19
	4	0	7
	5	0	0
	6	0	0
	7	0	0
2.12	1	31	0
	2	13	28
	3	1	12
	4	0	1
	5	0	0
	6	0	0
	7	0	0
2.142	1	33	0
	2	25	29
	3	2	22
	4	0	7
	5	0	0
	6	0	0
	7	0	0
2.141 (with stories)	1	31	0
	2	25	28
	3	3	21
	4	2	6
	5	1	3
	6	1	1
	7	0	2

on a given day. The numerical values of N_i are given in the presumed equilibrium distributions, Table 5.9.

The essential idea of the LOST models is that the expected number of arrivals to groups of size i in any short interval equals some function linear in i times the number $n_i(t)$ of groups of size i at the beginning of that interval. Summing over t,

$$E(A_i) = (a + bi)N_i, \tag{5.2}$$

and similarly for departures,

$$E(D_i) = diN_i. \tag{5.3}$$

A first ad hoc procedure for estimating a/d and b/d might be to divide (5.2) by (5.3). Then $E(A_i)/E(D_i) = (a/d)(1/i) + b/d$ is a linear function in $1/i$. Hence, by regressing against $1/i$ estimates of $E(A_i)/E(D_i)$, obtained by simply substituting A_i/D_i from Table 5.10, one would obtain estimates of a/d and b/d as the regression parameters.

However, this procedure throws away too much information, because it makes sense to calculate the ratio A_i/D_i only when both A_i and D_i are not zero. For 5 of the 6 sets of "good" data there are only two such values of i; for set 1.29 there are three. This procedure does not take advantage of the information contained in A_i or D_i for the larger values of i; for 5 sets of data, it prevents checking the assumption that A_i/D_i is linear in $1/i$. (If, nevertheless, estimates of a/d and b/d are calculated this way, they are found to differ wildly from the estimates obtained by fitting the equilibrium distribution.)

A second and preferable ad hoc procedure is to notice from (5.2) that $E(A_i)/N_i$ should be linear in i with intercept a and slope b and, similarly, from (5.3) that $E(D_i)/N_i$ should fall along a line through the origin with slope d. The regression coefficients a, b, and d estimated separately could then give the ratios a/d and b/d. This is the procedure actually used.

By way of illustration, Figure 5.1a gives a plot of A_i/N_i against i, where $i = 1$, 2, 3 for 27 January and the fitted regression line with intercept $a = 0.093$ and slope $b = 0.018$. Figure 5.1b gives a plot of D_i/N_i for $i = 2$, 3, 4 and a

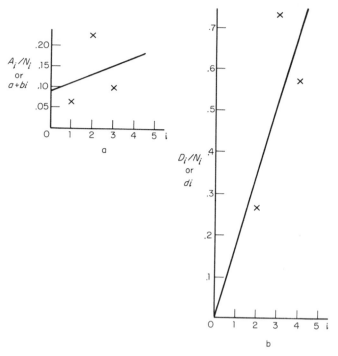

Figure 5.1a   Arrivals to groups of size i divided by the number of groups of size i, plotted as a function of i, for set 1.27.

Figure 5.1b   Departures from groups of size i divided by the number of groups of size i, plotted as a function of i, for set 1.27.

regression line through the origin with slope $d = 0.173$. Thus, on the basis of the dynamic data, the estimated parameters of the LOST model for that day are $a/d = 0.54$ and $b/d = 0.11$. The parameter values for the other days are presented in Table 5.11. In this table, on the days (2.12 and 2.142) when the equilibrium distribution could be described by the truncated Poisson distribution, the regression parameter b was set to zero; hence, the intercept of the horizontal line $a + bi$ was just the average over i of the values A_i/N_i.

The inelegance of this makeshift procedure for estimating a/d and b/d from the dynamic data is obvious. Explicit suggestions of better methods applicable to these data would be helpful.

Table 5.11. Estimated Arrival and Departure Parameters of Free Play of Four-Year-Olds at Cambridge Nursery School[a]

Set	Dynamic[b]					Brass (d = 1)	
	a	b	d	a/d	b/d	a	b
1.27	0.0933	0.0185	0.1731	0.539	0.107	0.256	0.214
1.28	0.0507	0.0264	0.2015	0.252	0.131	0.302	0.145
1.29	−0.0086	0.0646	0.3869	−0.023	0.175	0.417	0.191
2.7	0.0808	0.0104	0.1485	0.544	0.070	0.440	0.210
2.12	0.0754	0	0.1113	0.677	0	0.616	0
2.142	0.1008	0	0.2137	0.476	0	0.648	0
2.141	0.0798	0.0197	0.1677	0.476	0.117	0.057	0.492

[a]Estimations are based on 30-second intervals.
[b]The dimensions of a, b, and d are (half-minute) $^{-1}$; a/d and b/d are dimensionless.

The estimates of a, b, and d given in Table 5.11 make possible a reasonable guess about whether the play groups constitute an approximately equilibrial system for most of the period of observation (begun usually 15 minutes after the start of play) or whether most of what was observed was a transient. The guess is based on a rough comparison of the estimated parameters with those used to generate Table 4.2, the solution over time of the LOST equations (Section 4.4). The values $a = 1.2$, $b = 0.6$, and $d = 2.0$ used in Table 4.2 are about 10 times the rounded parameters $a = 0.1$, $b = 0.02$, and $d = 0.2$ estimated for set 1.27 or those estimated for set 2.142 ($a = 0.1$ and $d = 0.2$), which may be taken as typical. As shown in Section 4.4, the deterministic system of equations approached apparent equilibrium within half a time unit and very closely within one full time unit. Since the nursery system would be changing 10 times more slowly, it would, on the average, be expected to approach apparent equilibrium within 5 to 10 time units (30-second intervals), that is, within 5 minutes, even if initially the system consisted only of isolates. Hence, the much longer period of observation for each day may reasonably be taken to be at equilibrium.

Along with the dynamic estimates of a/d and b/d given in Table 5.11 are the equilibrium estimates derived from the values of r and p in Table 5.9 by the relations $a = r(1 - p)$

and $b = 1 - p$ (where $d = 1$ by convention). If the LOST models are correct in their dynamic details as well as in their equilibrium predictions, the two estimates of a/d should agree and the two estimates of b/d should agree. Because of the variability of the data and the imperfections of the estimators, the two kinds of estimates could not be expected to agree exactly. The problem is to measure the variability of each estimate with respect to each set of data and to establish a confidence interval at, say, the 95 percent level for the difference between the dynamic and the equilibrium estimates of a/d and b/d. If these confidence intervals include zero, then we cannot reject the assumption that the two estimators aim for the same quantity. The detailed dynamics of the LOST models would then not be disconfirmed, and they could be accepted for the time being as a simple description of the dynamics of nursery school play.

While Brass (1958) derived analytically the asymptotic variance and covariance of his estimators, a similar calculation for the dynamic estimators used here seems forbidding. Fortunately, a simple computational tool, the jackknife, makes it easy to compute numerically the variances of Brass's estimators and the dynamic estimators and, hence, of their differences and then to establish the desired confidence intervals by use of the t test. Information on the jackknife is easily accessible in the lucid presentation of Mosteller and Tukey (1968). The essential formulas, following Mosteller and Tukey, and the details of applying the technique to the nursery school data, are given in Appendix A to this chapter.

Table 5.12 summarizes the results of jackknifing the estimators and their differences and gives variances and 95 percent confidence intervals for each day's data separately. The jackknifed estimates of the parameters differ slightly from those given in Table 5.11; the bias-reducing properties of the jackknife probably make the estimates in Table 5.12 the more reliable. One difference in procedure between the two tables should be noted: whereas in Table 5.11, b was set to zero if the truncated Poisson could describe the equilibrium distribution, in Table 5.12, the fits to the equilibrium were not considered. Instead, the

Table 5.12. Jackknifed Ratios of Brass and Dynamic Estimates of LOST Parameters Based on Nursery School Data; Standard Deviations and 95 Percent Confidence Intervals (CI)

Set	Statistic	Jackknifed a/d			Jackknifed b/d		
		Brass[a]	Dynamic	Brass − dynamic[b]	Brass[a]	Dynamic	Brass − dynamic[b]
1.27	Parameter	.24	.51	−.27	.23	.13	.10
	s*[c]	.14	.19	.22	.10	.14	.13
	95%	−.09	.07	−.77	.01	−.18	−.19
	CI	.56	.94	.23	.45	.44	.39
1.28	Parameter	.28	.34	−.06	.16	.04	.12
	s*	.13	.26	.24	.09	.14	.10
	95%	−.02	−.26	−.60	−.05	−.27	−.10
	CI	.57	.94	.48	.38	.35	.34
1.29	Parameter	.31	.64	−.33	.27	−.60	.88
	s*	.19	.32	.49	.14	.41	.54
	95%	−.12	−.09	−1.43	−.05	−1.53	−.33
	CI	.75	1.37	.78	.59	.32	2.09
2.7	Parameter	.43	.57	−.14	.21	.09	.12
	s*	.11	.27	.33	.07	.13	.14
	95%	.18	−.03	−.89	.05	−.20	−.20
	CI	.69	1.17	.62	.38	.38	.45
2.12	Parameter	.61	.63	−.02	0	0	0
	s*	.08	.14	.12	0	0	0
	95%	.43	.32	−.28	0	0	0
	CI	.80	.95	.24	0	0	0
2.142	Parameter	.54	.50	.04	.07	−.03	.10
(without	s*	.11	.21	.25	.05	.09	.10
stories)	95%	.29	.02	−.52	−.03	−.22	−.13
	CI	.79	.98	.60	.17	.17	.32
2.141	Parameter	−2.49	−.95	−1.54	2.13	.45	1.68
(with	s*	1.05	.57	.49	.67	.17	.55
stories)	95%	−4.86	−2.23	−2.66	.61	.06	.44
	CI	−.12	.34	−.42	3.64	.84	2.92

[a]Negative lower limits of the CI for the Brass estimates should be adjusted upward to zero (see Appendix A to Chapter 5).

[b]The CI of the difference of the two estimates include zero if the two do not differ significantly.

[c]In this and subsequent tables s* stands for standard deviation.

mean and variance of that distribution were checked against Sampford's (1955) criterion (A2.8), and both parameters a and b were calculated from the data if the criterion was met. Only if the criterion was not met was b set to zero for both the Brass and dynamic estimates. Then the maximum likelihood estimate of the parameter of the truncated Poisson was calculated iteratively to an absolute accuracy of not less than 10^{-3}.

The only difference this makes is in set 2.142 (not including storytelling); instead of Brass parameters $a = 0.65$, $b = 0$ and dynamic parameters $a/d = 0.48$, $b/d = 0$, we have jackknifed Brass parameters $a = 0.54$, $b = 0.07$ and dynamic parameters $a/d = 0.50$ and $b/d = -0.03$. According to the jackknifed variances in Table 5.12, neither estimate of b is distinguishable from zero, even though neither was forced to be zero.

The lower and upper limits of the 95 percent confidence interval (CI) of the differences between the Brass (equilibrium) and dynamic estimates of a/d and b/d are given in Table 5.12 in the lower right corner of the block of twelve statistics calculated for each parameter for each day. For example, the 95 percent confidence interval around $-.27$, the difference between the jackknifed Brass and dynamic estimates of a/d in set 1.27, is $(-.77, +.23)$. As long as these limits include zero, the dynamics of the LOST model are compatible with the data. As the table shows, for all six sets of "good" data, the confidence intervals of the differences do include zero. The model does fail, as desired, for set 2.141, in which the formation of groups around a storyteller clearly upset the dynamics assumed to be at work.

This startling (to me) success of the LOST models suggests that it would be fruitful to test the models' other assumptions about the details of dynamics. One of the most important of these is that the rates of arrival to and departure from groups of size greater than 1 are independent of the number of isolates in the system. With greater foresight, the calculations for this test could have been built into the same computer routine used to compare the dynamic and equilibrial parameter estimates; but for logistical reasons, only sample calculations on data set 1.27 are reported here. It seems reasonable to presume that the other days' data would not differ substantially.

For data set 1.27, the number of isolates at each epoch was correlated with the number of arrivals to groups of size 2 that occurred between that epoch and the next. To the nearest 0.01, the correlation was 0.01. The number of isolates at each epoch was also correlated with the number of departures from groups of size 2 which occurred between that epoch and the next. To the nearest 0.01, the correlation was −0.09. In both cases, the procedure used for counting arrivals and departures was the same as that used to make the histograms of arrivals and departures. Neither calculated correlation remotely approaches the 0.05 or the 0.95 percentiles of the sampling distribution of the correlation under the assumption that the two variables are independent (and normally distributed, which is at least approximately true); to the nearest 0.01, these values for a sample size of 88 are (−0.18, +0.18). Thus, the correlation of the number of isolates with arrivals to or departures from pairs is not significant at the 10 percent level.

Similar correlations should be calculated for arrivals to and departures from groups of other sizes and for other sets of data. But enough detailed assumptions of the LOST models have already been found compatible with the data to make it worth reconsidering how seriously the details of the LOST dynamics can be taken.

As noted in Section 4.1, under some circumstances (with an abundance of isolates) the LOST models could be expected to approximate more plausible nonlinear models. In a closed system of groups with no isolates, it is clearly impossible for the closed LOST model to hold; in the next small interval of time, groups larger than 1 could not possibly increase by 1. Hence, if LOST dynamics are at all credible it must be when they are embedded in some open model. Whether that open model is the one described in Section 4.3 or some other, there must be a sufficient flow of isolates into the system from the environment to guarantee the necessary flow of arrivals to larger groups. Thus, the truth of the LOST dynamics is conditional on the providence of the environment. If the parameters of a given system guarantee many isolates, then few demands will

95

be made on that providence. Otherwise, closure of entry into a system should guarantee the failure of LOST dynamics.

In conclusion, although the LOST models do not robustly describe all situations of social mixing—and can be thrown off by as simple a form of social organization as a storytelling group—in a situation where casual groups are truly freely forming, they do seem to describe both the equilibrium distribution of group sizes and the dynamics of group formation.

C. Frederick Mosteller has privately raised the interesting question: Is the variability, from day to day in nursery school play, of the parameters by which the LOST models characterize group formation greater than could be accounted for simply by the small size of the daily sample of observations, or is the variability about the same as might be expected? Appendix B to this chapter indicates that the variability of the parameter ratios a/d and b/d is about the same as would be expected from an underlying LOST process with parameters that are constant from day to day. Therefore, the data do not contradict the assumption, over the few weeks of observation, of constant rates of arrivals to and departures from play groups.

5.5 How Open Is This Open System?

In the theoretical open system described in Section 4.3, all individuals leaving groups of a size greater than 2 quit the system, and those joining groups of a size greater than 1 join the system from outside. Clearly, the observed system of nursery school play groups is not so open as this. But neither is it sealed off like the closed theoretical system described in Section 4.1. This section proposes a measure of the closure or degree of closedness of a system of groups based on an analogy with the hydraulic concept of detention time, and it applies this measure to the theoretical and observed systems of groups.

The detention time (DT) of a system that contains a fluid and through which there is also a steady flow of that fluid is simply the volume of fluid in the system divided by the rate of flow (into or out of the system, since the volume in the system is assumed to be steady). Thus, if a tank holding two gallons is receiving a steady flow of one gallon an hour, the detention time of the system is two hours.

If the fluid in the system is perfectly mixed, the detention time measures the average time during which fluid remains in the system. If fluid passes through the system in "plug flow," as if the particles of fluid were marching through in single file, the detention time again measures the fluid's average duration of stay in the system; in this case the variance of the duration is zero (assuming steady flow and volume). If part of the volume of the system is "dead space" occupied by fluid that is not flowing, then the average duration of stay of particles that do flow through the system is shorter than the theoretical detention time calculated as the ratio of volume to flow.

In the nursery school playroom, the volume of the system may be taken as the average number of individuals in it at any instant. The rate of flow through the system may be taken as the average of the average number of entries to the system per minute and the average number of exits from the system per minute. The ratio of the volume to the flow then gives a theoretical detention time in minutes.

The children's entries to and exits from the playroom were clearly not plug flow. Because the individual identities of the children entering and leaving were not recorded, there is no solid evidence to show whether the flow differed significantly from perfect mixing, though informal observation suggests that some children found more excuses to enter and leave the room than others. Without prejudice about the actual amount of mixing, we now calculate the theoretical and observed detention times of the playroom (making no allowance for children who always remain in the room).

For the closed theoretical system of Section 4.1, the detention time is infinite. For the open theoretical system of Section 4.3, where the expectation is over time, the detention time,

$$DT = \frac{E[N(t)]}{E(\text{flow})}, \qquad (5.4)$$

may be calculated with the aid of (4.15), with the term containing $c = 0$ omitted:

$$\frac{dN(t)}{dt} = an(t) + bN(t) - d[N(t) - n_1(t)]. \qquad (5.5)$$

The first two terms on the right are entries to the system, and the last term represents exits from the system. Therefore, the expected net flow through the system at equilibrium is simply

$$E(\text{flow}) = \frac{aE[n(t)] + (b+d)E[N(t)] - dE[n_1(t)]}{2} \qquad (5.6)$$

which is just one half the expectation of the right side of (5.5), with the sign in front of d changed from minus to plus.

The detention times of theoretical open systems having the parameters estimated for nursery school play may be calculated from (5.4) and (5.6), remembering that the parameter values of a, b, and d in Table 5.11 are in units of (30-seconds)$^{-1}$. The histograms in Table 5.9 easily yield $E[n(t)]$, $E[N(t)]$, and $E[n_1(t)]$. Since the average over time appears in both the numerator and denominator of (5.4), in actual calculation these three quantities may be replaced, respectively, by the total number of groups observed throughout the observation peiod, the total number of individuals observed, and the total number of isolates observed. The theoretical detention times, in minutes, of open systems having the parameters estimated from each day's observations are listed in Table 5.13, second column from the right.

To find the actual detention times of the systems of nursery school play groups, the theoretical flow in the denominator of (5.4) is replaced by an estimate of actual flow into and out of the system. From the data (Tables 5.1–5.7), an entry to the system was inferred each time the number of individuals in the system increased by 1, and an exit was inferred each time the number of individuals in the system decreased by 1. For example, in the transition between epochs 4 and 5 of set 1.27, the number of individuals in the system went from 8 to 9, and a single entry was inferred. It is possible that actually all 8 individuals in the system at epoch 4 left and 9 new individuals entered

Table 5.13. Detention Times of Observed Systems of Nursery School Play Compared With Detention Times of Theoretical Open Systems Having the Same Parameters

Set	Entries	Exits	Epochs	Individuals	Groups	Actual detention time (minutes)	Theoretical detention time (minutes)	Closure index[a]
1.27	12	11	89	780	598	33.532	6.209	5.400
1.28	7	7	101	807	635	57.072	6.971	8.187
1.29	9	9	78	762	548	41.791	4.027	10.377
2.7	20	17	95	900	625	24.068	6.990	3.443
2.12	5	3	82	718	536	88.655	9.267	9.567
2.142	26	20	85	892	657	19.163	5.727	3.346
2.141	14	8	85	1006	679	45.189	6.157	7.339

[a]Ratio of actual to theoretical detention times.

by epoch 5, at least according to the data alone. That, however, was not what happened, and the inference to single entries and exits is correct. The second and third columns of Table 5.13 give the numbers of entries and exits during each period of observation. The rate of flow is the average of these numbers, divided by the time of observation. The time of observation, in minutes, is the number of epochs of observation less 1, all divided by 2. Thus, the actual detention time in minutes is

$$DT = \frac{(\text{total no. of individuals/total no. of epochs})}{(\text{no. of entries} + \text{no. of exits})/(\text{total no. of epochs} - 1)} \ (\text{min.}). \quad (5.7)$$

Table 5.13 gives the total number of epochs, individuals, and groups observed each day and the actual detention time based on (5.7). In each case, the actual detention time is considerably greater than that of a theoretical open system with the same parameters; the median detention time is approximately the amount of time planned for any single kind of activity for the children during the nursery school day. Thus, under perfect mixing or plug flow, during any single activity period, each child could be expected to enter and leave the playroom approximately once.

Appendix A to Chapter 5: The Jackknife and Its Application

"The jackknife offers ways to set sensible confidence limits in complex situations," according to Mosteller and Tukey (1968:134). The bare bones of the technique, as they present it, along with my way of applying it to the nursery school data, are presented in this appendix.

The goal is to assess the variance of any statistic y (such as the Brass estimate of a or the dynamic estimate of a/d or their difference) with respect to a given sample of data (such as one day's nursery school observations). Suppose the sample is divided into some number k of blocks of observations. Let $y_{(j)}$ be the value of the statistic obtained on the basis of all observations in the sample *except* those in the jth block, that is, with the jth block *omitted*. Let y_{all} be the statistic calculated on the basis of the whole sample. Then pseudovalues are defined as

$$y_{*j} = ky_{\text{all}} - (k-1)y_{(j)}, \qquad j = 1, 2, \ldots, k. \qquad \text{(A5.1)}$$

The jackknifed estimate, the "best single result," is then given by

$$y_* = \frac{y_{*1} + \cdots + y_{*k}}{k} \qquad \text{(A5.2)}$$

and an estimate of its variance is given by

$$s_*^2 = \frac{\Sigma y_{*j}^2 - (\Sigma y_{*j})^2/k}{k(k-1)}. \qquad \text{(A5.3)}$$

Mosteller and Tukey (1968:136–138) adjoin various admonitions to this simple calculation, which have been heeded but will not be repeated here. According to their rule of thumb, the df for the value of t used to find the confidence interval are one less than the number of different numbers that appear as pseudovalues.

Application of this technique to the first day's data, set 1.27, will illustrate the mechanized procedure used with

100

all the days. The number of blocks chosen was $k = 10$. The 89 epochs were divided as evenly as possible into 10 successive blocks by rounding successive multiples of 89/10 to the nearest integer and using these numbers as the last epoch of blocks.

To jackknife the equilibrium estimates, the histogram of group sizes within each block was subtracted from the histogram of group sizes for the whole sample. Brass's estimates of $p_{(j)}$ and $r_{(j)}$ were then calculated for each of the reduced histograms and were immediately transformed to $a_{(j)} = r_{(j)}q_{(j)}$ and $b_{(j)} = q_{(j)}$. The jackknife was then applied directly to a and to b, not to Brass's estimates of p and r. The calculations were carried out with eight significant figures, but for illustration here they are rounded to three significant figures. The full sample estimates of a and b were:

$$a_{all} = 0.256 \quad b_{all} = 0.214.$$

(These parameters were calculated using Fortran IV on the IBM 7094; the same estimates in Table 5.9 were calculated from an independent program written in CAL on the SDS 940 time-sharing system. That the corresponding estimates do not differ by more than 3×10^{-8} gives confidence that both computing systems are finding the same quantities.) The estimates of $a_{(j)}$ and $b_{(j)}$ in order of block omitted were:

j	$a_{(j)}$	$b_{(j)}$
1	0.269	0.220
2	.246	.225
3	.259	.213
4	.256	.219
5	.274	.208
6	.298	.191
7	.265	.224
8	.348	.129
9	.159	.256
10	.208	.240

The pseudovalues calculated from (A5.1) were:

j	a_{*j}	b_{*j}
1	0.135	0.160
2	.351	.114
3	.231	.224
4	.256	.171
5	.097	.266
6	− .120	.422
7	.176	.123
8	− .575	.981
9	1.133	− .164
10	.692	− .025

Even though a and b must be positive, some of the pseudovalues are negative. This does not present any problem since the bulk of the pseudovalues lies within the permissible range. The difficulty could be avoided entirely by jackknifing suitably transformed statistics and then applying the inverse transform, as Mosteller and Tukey suggest. But the variance under the transformation will not in general inversely transform into the variance in the original scale of a and b, which is of interest here. So the few negative pseudovalues are accepted, and the lower end of the confidence interval should be pushed up to zero when the calculation indicates a negative value.

From (A5.2), the jackknifed equilibrium estimates of a and b are:

$$a_* = 0.238 \quad b_* = 0.227.$$

From (A5.3) the corresponding standard deviations are:

$$s_*(a) = 0.143 \quad s_*(b) = 0.098.$$

Since ten numerically different pseudovalues were obtained for both a and b, the 95 percent confidence interval around $a_* = 0.238$ is $0.238 \pm |t_9|_{.95} \times s_*(a) = 0.238 \pm$ (2.262)(0.143), or the interval (calculated with unrounded figures) from −0.086 to 0.561, which we correct to the interval from zero to 0.561. Similarly, the 95 percent confidence interval around $b_* = 0.227$ is $0.227 \pm (2.262)(0.098)$, or the interval (calculated with unrounded figures) from

0.007 to 0.448. These jackknifed estimates, standard deviations, and confidence limits appear in Table 5.12.

To jackknife the dynamic estimates of a/d and b/d, the histogram by group size of arrivals and departures was calculated for the epochs within each block (neglecting the transition from the last epoch of one block to the first epoch of the next block). The histogram for each block was subtracted from the histogram for the whole sample to give the histograms by group size of arrivals and departures with each block omitted. The dynamic estimates of a, b, and d were then calculated from these reduced histograms of arrivals and departures and from the corresponding reduced histograms of group sizes (obtained in the parallel computation of the Brass parameters with each block omitted). The ratios of the parameters $(a/d)_{(j)}$ and $(b/d)_{(j)}$, and not the separate parameters a, b, and d, were then put into the jackknife to obtain the dynamic estimates, standard deviations, and confidence intervals summarized in Table 5.12.

This procedure of first calculating the necessary histograms or frequency distributions for the whole sample and then subtracting the histograms corresponding to the block omitted required only two passes through the data instead of ten. The entire procedure could have been done in one pass at the expense of devoting greater memory to the block histograms while the overall histograms were being cumulated.

All the jackknife calculations on nursery school play reported here were carried out on the IBM 7094 in less than two minutes, after approximately one minute of loading and compiling a Fortran IV deck. In this problem, programming is by far the most expensive part of the technique.

Appendix B to Chapter 5: Stochastic Simulation and Parameter Stability

This section describes the construction and output of a fully stochastic simulation of the LOST process. By means described in Section B5.1 and using constant parameters, this simulation generated 600 epochs of "observations." Section B5.2 analyzes the equilibrium distributions of group sizes obtained by treating these observations as if they were real. Section B5.3 applies the jackknife to these observations as in Appendix A to this chapter. Section B5.4, which is the point of the exercise, shows that the variability in the LOST parameters estimated from one simulated "day of observation" to another is not detectably different from the apparent variability from day to day in the parameters estimated from the observations of nursery school play.

The question answered in Section B5.4 arises because, for example, in Table 5.12, the jackknifed estimate of a/d on 27 January, 0.24, lies outside the 95 percent confidence interval (0.29, 0.79) of the estimate 0.54 of the parameter a/d on 14 February (excluding stories); similarly for b/d on those two dates. This section suggests that such apparent variability in the parameters could result simply from the short duration of observation on each day and is consistent with constant underlying parameters.

B5.1 The Simulation

In a discrete-time stochastic simulation of the LOST models, the defining equations (4.1) or (A4.1) for $i = 2, 3, \ldots$ take the form

$$n_i(t + 1) = [n_i(t) + X_{1i}(t) - X_{2i}(t)]^+, \qquad (B5.1)$$

where $(y)^+ = y$ if $y \geq 0$; $(y)^+ = 0$ if $y \leq 0$; $n_i(t)$ is the number of groups of size i at epoch t; $t = 1, 2, \ldots, 600$; $X_{1i}(t)$ is a Poisson variate with mean and variance equal to

$$[a + b(i - 1)]n_{i-1}(t) + d(i + 1)n_{i+1}(t), \qquad (B5.2)$$

and $X_{2i}(t)$ is a Poisson variate with mean and variance equal to

$$[a + (b + d)i]n_i(t), \qquad (B5.3)$$

and all the Poisson variates are mutually independent. It is necessary to impose positivity on the right side of (B5.1) because it is possible for $X_{2i}(t)$ to be greater than $n_i(t) +$

$X_{1i}(t)$. In fact, in the course of generating 599 epochs from the initial epoch given below, positivity had to be imposed 52 times: 28 times for $i = 2$; 19 times for $i = 3$; 4 times for $i = 4$; and once for $i = 5$. I have not explored the theory of this distribution.

Of the variety of possible ways of specifying $n_1(t)$ I chose to calculate $n_2(t)$, $n_3(t)$, . . . , for each new epoch t by (B5.1) and then take $n_1(t)$ as

$$n_1(t) = \left[10 - \sum_2^{10} in_i(t) \right]^+. \tag{B5.4}$$

This definition guarantees 10 or more individuals in the system at all times. When there are more than 10 individuals, there are no isolates; groups that increase in size do so by attracting single individuals directly from outside the system. The system contained exactly 10 individuals for 571 of the 600 epochs simulated.

In order to make the state vector $[n_1(t), n_2(t), . . . ,]$ of the system finite-dimensional, I took $n_i(t) = 0$, for $i > 10$. This truncation turned out to be generous, since with the parameters adopted the largest group simulated was of size 5. The simulation began with 10 isolates, $n_1(1) = 10$.

To generate random values from a Poisson distribution with parameter λ from the random variate U with a uniform distribution on $(0, 1)$ that was available within the computer, I found the least k such that

$$U \leq \sum_{j=0}^{k} \frac{e^{-\lambda}\lambda^j}{j!}. \tag{B5.5}$$

Since in this simulation λ was typically less than 2 or 3 and the testing for the minimal k could be coded efficiently, this brute Poisson inversion was not too expensive. Larger λ would require a more sophisticated procedure.

From the $n_i(t)$, a vector of simulated group sizes was automatically generated so that the output of the simulation could be treated in the same way as the real data. The 6 sets of 100 epochs each are listed in continuous sequence in Table B5.4 at the end of this appendix, without separate numbering. Set 7 will refer to all 600 blocks taken together as one sequence of observations.

105

The values of a, b, and d used to carry out the simulation were the respective means of the values of a, b, and d given for the first 6 sets in Table 5.11 (excluding set 2.141, Valentine's Day with stories), weighted by the number of epochs of observation on each day (given in Table 5.13). The values obtained were $a = 0.066378$, $b = 0.019509$, and $d = 0.202517$, giving parameter ratios $a/d = 0.327765$ and $b/d = 0.096333$.

B5.2 Equilibrium Distributions

The frequency distributions of group size based on the simulated data of Table B5.4 appear in Table B5.1. By the criterion of the χ^2 test, all 7 sets of data in Table B5.1 could have been fitted by the truncated Poisson distribution, although the fit to set 4 would have been rejected at the 5 percent level. These fits show that when the true parameter b/d is positive but small, short periods of observation may appear consistent with the assumption that $b/d = 0$. In fact, the sampling fluctuations in two of the sets of data (2 and 5) were such that the Sampford conditions (A2.8) on the moments of a truncated negative binomial distribution were not met. (In Table 5.9, giving the equilibrium group size distributions of the nursery observations, set 2.12 failed to meet the Sampford conditions; set 2.142 did meet those conditions but was adequately described by the truncated Poisson.) Both simulated sets 2 and 5 were well described by the truncated Poisson, according to the criterion of the χ^2 test.

Thus, the group size distributions of the simulated sets were consistent with the equilibrium predictions of the LOST models, although the estimated parameters varied considerably, as Table B5.1 shows. After applying the jackknife to each set of data, we will return to this variability in estimated parameters.

B5.3 The Jackknife

Table B5.2 gives the results of applying the jackknife (Appendix A to this chapter) to each set of simulated data in exactly the same way it was applied to the real data (Sec-

Table B5.1. Frequency Distributions of Group Size in LOST Simulation[a]

Set	Group size	Observed frequency	Predicted frequency	Truncated negative binomial	Truncated Poisson
1	1	686	685.8	$p = 0.978$	$\lambda = a = 0.394$
	2	132	132.9	$r = 16.422$	$x^2 = 0.164$
	3	19	18.1	$a = 0.365$	df = 2
	≥4	2	2.2	$b = 0.022$	$0.9 < P < 0.95$
				$x^2 = 0.057$	
				df = 1	
				$0.8 < P < 0.9$	
2	1	535	536.0	(failed	$\lambda = a = 0.671$
	2	180	179.9	Sampford	$x^2 = 0.645$
	3	43	40.3	criterion)	df = 3
	4	5	6.8		$0.8 < P < 0.9$
	≥5	1	1.0		
3	1	627	625.9	$p = 0.942$	$\lambda = a = 0.482$
	2	138	144.1	$r = 6.930$	$x^2 = 4.049$
	3	32	24.9	$a = 0.402$	df = 2
	≥4	2	4.1	$b = 0.058$	$0.1 < P < 0.2$
				$x^2 = 3.359$	
				df = 1	
				$0.05 < P < 0.10$	
4	1	620	618.4	$p = 0.883$	$\lambda = a = 0.521$
	2	139	147.3	$r = 3.080$	$x^2 = 6.577$
	3	38	29.1	$a = 0.360$	df = 2
	≥4	4	6.2	$b = 0.117$	$0.02 < P < 0.05$
				$x^2 = 3.950$	
				df = 1	
				$0.02 < P < 0.05$	
5	1	702	707.3	(failed	$\lambda = a = 0.352$
	2	132	124.6	Sampford	$x^2 = 2.487$
	3	10	14.6	criterion)	df = 2
	≥4	2	1.4		$0.2 < P < 0.3$
6	1	562	561.0	$p = 0.922$	$\lambda = a = 0.596$
	2	153	157.4	$r = 6.234$	$x^2 = 1.924$
	3	37	33.5	$a = 0.483$	df = 2
	≥4	7	7.1	$b = 0.078$	$0.3 < P < 0.5$
				$x^2 = 0.492$	
				df = 1	
				$0.3 < P < 0.5$	
Sum of 1-6	1	3732	3728.3	$p = 0.943$	$\lambda = a = 0.501$
	2	876	894.5	$r = 7.446$	$x^2 = 7.785$
	3	179	160.0	$a = 0.423$	df = 3
	4	22	23.7	$b = 0.057$	$0.05 < P < 0.10$
	≥5	1	3.5	$x^2 = 4.550$	
				df = 2	
				$0.1 < P < 0.2$	

[a]Parameters: $a/d = 0.327765$, $b/d = 0.096333$.

Table B5.2. Jackknifed Ratios of Brass and Dynamic Estimates of LOST Parameters Based on the LOST Simulation,[a] Standard Deviation and 95 Percent Confidence Intervals(CI)

		Jackknifed a/d			Jackknifed b/d		
Set	Statistic	Brass[b]	Dynamic	Brass − dynamic[c]	Brass[b]	Dynamic	Brass − dynamic[c]
1	Parameter	0.37	0.75	−0.38	0.02	−0.37	0.39
	s*	0.12	0.26	0.33	0.07	0.11	0.17
	95%	0.10	0.15	−1.14	−0.14	−0.63	−0.001
	CI	0.63	1.34	0.37	0.18	−0.12	0.78
2	Parameter	0.72	0.62	0.11	−0.04	−0.13	0.09
	s*	0.15	0.24	0.28	0.03	0.09	0.06
	95%	0.38	0.08	−0.53	−0.10	−0.32	−0.05
	CI	1.07	1.15	0.74	0.03	0.07	0.24
3	Parameter	0.36	0.20	0.16	0.09	−0.11	0.20
	s*	0.12	0.26	0.25	0.08	0.06	0.12
	95%	0.10	−0.38	−0.41	−0.10	−0.25	−0.07
	CI	0.62	0.79	0.72	0.27	0.04	0.46
4	Parameter	0.32	0.39	−0.07	0.14	−0.03	0.17
	s*	0.18	0.27	0.17	0.07	0.07	0.04
	95%	−0.08	−0.22	−0.46	−0.02	−0.18	0.08
	CI	0.73	1.00	0.33	0.29	0.12	0.26
5	Parameter	0.38	0.63	−0.25	−0.01	−0.07	0.06
	s*	0.07	0.28	0.23	0.01	0.07	0.06
	95%	0.22	−0.01	−0.77	−0.05	−0.23	−0.07
	CI	0.54	1.26	0.27	0.02	0.09	0.18
6	Parameter	0.45	0.44	0.01	0.10	0.00	0.09
	s*	0.21	0.24	0.19	0.11	0.10	0.08
	95%	−0.01	−0.11	−0.42	−0.16	−0.23	−0.08
	CI	0.92	0.99	0.44	0.35	0.24	0.27
Sum	Parameter	0.42	0.37	0.05	0.06	−0.11	0.17
of	s*	0.05	0.08	0.11	0.03	0.03	0.05
1-6	95%	0.31	0.18	−0.20	−0.01	−0.17	0.06
	CI	0.53	0.56	0.29	0.13	−0.05	0.28

[a]Simulation parameters: a/d = 0.327765, b/d = 0.096333.

[b]Negative lower limits of the CI for the Brass estimates should be adjusted upward to zero (see Appendix A to Chapter 5).

[c]The CI of the difference of the two estimators includes zero if the two do not differ significantly.

tion 5.4, where the corresponding results appear in Table 5.12). The simulated histograms of arrivals and departures by group size corresponding to Table 5.10 are omitted here.

The jackknifed Brass and dynamic estimates of a/d and b/d vary considerably. For example, the jackknifed Brass estimate in set 4 of a/d (0.32) lies outside the 95 percent confidence interval (0.38, 1.07) estimated by the jackknife for a/d in set 2. Similarly, the jackknifed dynamic estimate of b/d in set 1 (−0.37) lies outside the 95 percent confidence interval (−0.18, 0.12) estimated for b/d in set 4. There are many additional examples, even though all the data were generated from a process with constant parameters.

All of the 95 percent confidence intervals around the jackknifed difference between the Brass and dynamic estimates of a/d include zero, as they should if the Brass and dynamic estimators are aiming for the same quantity. For b/d, the confidence intervals around the difference of the Brass and dynamic estimators fail to include zero in set 4 and set 7. Since the parameters of the simulation are known, these failures show that small-sample fluctuations may combine with the shortcomings of the estimators (particularly the dynamic estimators) to indicate rejection of the LOST dynamics when the LOST dynamics are actually at work.

The converse error—acceptance of the LOST dynamics when other dynamics are actually at work—is a possibility that has been adumbrated only qualitatively near the end of Section 5.4.

These two failures in sets 4 and 7 excepted, the application of the jackknife to the Brass and dynamic estimates of the parameters gives the expected results when the data are known to be generated by a LOST process.

B5.4 Parameter Variability

To compare the variability from day to day in parameter estimates based on the nursery school observations with the variability from set to set of the parameter estimates based on the simulation, I calculated the variances of the equilibrium estimates of a/d and b/d (using Brass's estimators) and of the jackknifed Brass and dynamic estimates of a/d and b/d separately for the observed and simulated data. These variances appear in Table B5.3.

If the 6 observations (each observation being a parameter estimate based on a set of data) that contribute to each variance in Table B5.3 are approximately normally distributed, then the ratio of the variance of the estimates based on nursery school observations to the variance of the estimates based on simulated data should have the F distribution, if the variability in real data equals that in simulated data with constant parameters. The application of the F test to the ratios given in Table B5.3 shows that the variability from day to day of real parameter estimates does not differ from the variability from set to set of simulated parameter estimates, at the 5 percent level.

Table B5.3. Ratios *(F)* of Variances of Statistics Estimated First From Nursery School Data and Then From LOST Simulation

	Parameter *a/d*			Parameter *b/d*		
	Observed variance	Simulated variance	F^a	Observed variance	Simulated variance	F^a
Equilibrium[b]	0.025	0.015	1.66	0.010	0.002	4.64
Jackknifed Brass[c]	0.023	0.022	1.05	0.011	0.005	2.14
Jackknifed Dynamic[c]	0.012	0.040	0.31	0.073	0.018	4.16

[a]Assuming normality, a ratio outside the interval $(F(6,6)_{.025}, F(6,6)_{.975}) = (0.172, 5.82)$ indicates a difference in variance at the 5 percent level.

[b]From Tables 5.2 and B5.1.

[c]From Tables 5.4 and B5.2.

Hence, all the observations of nursery school play over a period of two and a half weeks could have been generated by a LOST process with constant parameters.

The simulated data on which this conclusion is based follow as Table B5.4.

Table B5.4 Simulated Data From a LOST Process With Constant Parameters

Epoch	Groups	Individuals	Sizes of groups	Epoch	Groups	Individuals	Sizes of groups
1	10	10	1111111111	46	9	10	211111111
2	10	10	1111111111	47	9	10	211111111
3	10	10	1111111111	48	10	10	1111111111
4	10	10	1111111111	49	9	10	211111111
5	10	10	1111111111	50	10	10	1111111111
6	10	10	1111111111	51	10	10	1111111111
7	10	10	1111111111	52	9	10	211111111
8	10	10	1111111111	53	8	10	22111111
9	10	10	1111111111	54	7	10	2221111
10	9	10	211111111	55	10	10	1111111111
11	10	10	1111111111	56	8	10	22111111
12	9	10	211111111	57	10	10	1111111111
13	9	10	211111111	58	9	10	211111111
14	8	10	31111111	59	7	10	3211111
15	8	10	31111111	60	7	10	2221111
16	5	10	32221	61	7	10	2221111
17	7	10	3211111	62	8	10	22111111
18	5	12	33222	63	7	10	2221111
19	7	10	2221111	64	8	10	22111111
20	8	10	22111111	65	8	10	22111111
21	9	10	211111111	66	8	10	22111111
22	10	10	1111111111	67	9	10	211111111
23	9	10	211111111	68	9	10	211111111
24	9	10	211111111	69	8	10	22111111
25	9	10	211111111	70	10	10	1111111111
26	8	10	22111111	71	9	10	211111111
27	8	10	22111111	72	9	10	211111111
28	9	10	211111111	73	8	10	22111111
29	10	10	1111111111	74	7	10	3211111
30	10	10	1111111111	75	9	10	211111111
31	7	10	2221111	76	10	10	1111111111
32	5	11	32222	77	10	10	1111111111
33	7	10	2221111	78	8	10	22111111
34	9	10	211111111	79	10	10	1111111111
35	8	10	22111111	80	7	10	2221111
36	8	10	22111111	81	6	10	322111
37	8	10	22111111	82	6	10	322111
38	8	10	31111111	83	8	10	22111111
39	6	15	432222	84	10	10	1111111111
40	7	17	4322222	85	10	10	1111111111
41	4	10	3322	86	8	10	22111111
42	6	10	322111	87	8	10	22111111
43	10	10	1111111111	88	10	10	1111111111
44	9	10	211111111	89	8	10	22111111
45	9	10	211111111	90	9	10	211111111

Table B5.4 (Continued)

Epoch	Groups	Indi-viduals	Sizes of groups	Epoch	Groups	Indi-viduals	Sizes of groups
91	8	10	22111111	136	8	10	22111111
92	8	10	22111111	137	6	10	222211
93	6	10	322111	138	6	10	222211
94	5	10	32221	139	7	10	3211111
95	8	10	22111111	140	8	10	22111111
96	7	10	2221111	141	9	10	211111111
97	8	10	22111111	142	8	10	22111111
98	9	10	211111111	143	7	10	2221111
99	10	10	1111111111	144	8	10	22111111
100	9	10	211111111	145	5	10	33211
101	8	10	22111111	146	8	10	22111111
102	5	10	33211	147	10	10	1111111111
103	5	13	43222	148	9	10	211111111
104	6	15	333222	149	6	10	322111
105	5	12	42222	150	9	10	211111111
< 106	3	10	532	151	6	10	322111
107	8	10	31111111	152	8	10	22111111
108	7	10	3211111	153	7	10	2221111
109	7	10	2221111	154	9	10	211111111
110	7	10	2221111	155	9	10	211111111
111	6	12	222222	156	7	10	2221111
112	6	15	333222	157	6	10	222211
113	4	11	3332	158	5	11	32222
114	5	10	33211	159	6	10	222211
115	6	14	332222	160	9	10	211111111
116	8	23	44333222	161	10	10	1111111111
117	8	18	33222222	162	7	10	2221111
118	7	10	2221111	163	10	10	1111111111
< 119	5	10	32221	164	9	10	211111111
120	10	10	1111111111	165	8	10	22111111
121	9	10	211111111	166	7	10	2221111
122	10	10	1111111111	167	10	10	1111111111
123	10	10	1111111111	168	8	10	22111111
124	7	10	2221111	169	9	10	211111111
125	9	10	211111111	170	9	10	211111111
126	10	10	1111111111	171	7	10	2221111
127	8	10	22111111	172	10	10	1111111111
128	6	10	322111	173	10	10	1111111111
129	8	10	31111111	174	9	10	211111111
130	8	10	22111111	175	7	10	2221111
131	8	10	22111111	176	9	10	211111111
132	9	10	211111111	177	7	10	2221111
133	8	10	22111111	178	7	10	3211111
134	8	10	22111111	179	9	10	211111111
135	9	10	211111111	180	10	10	1111111111

112

Epoch	Groups	Indi-viduals	Sizes of groups	Epoch	Groups	Indi-viduals	Sizes of groups
181	9	10	211111111	226	7	10	2221111
182	8	10	22111111	227	9	10	211111111
183	8	10	22111111	228	10	10	1111111111
184	8	10	22111111	229	10	10	1111111111
185	9	10	211111111	230	9	10	211111111
186	10	10	1111111111	231	9	10	211111111
187	9	10	211111111	232	8	10	22111111
188	9	10	211111111	233	9	10	211111111
189	9	10	211111111	234	7	10	2221111
190	8	10	22111111	235	9	10	211111111
191	9	10	211111111	236	10	10	1111111111
192	6	10	322111	237	10	10	1111111111
193	6	15	333222	238	9	10	211111111
194	5	10	22222	239	9	10	211111111
195	7	10	2221111	240	9	10	211111111
196	8	10	22111111	241	9	10	211111111
197	4	10	3331	242	10	10	1111111111
198	5	10	42211	243	10	10	1111111111
199	6	10	331111	244	9	10	211111111
200	10	10	1111111111	245	9	10	211111111
201	8	10	22111111	246	9	10	211111111
202	8	10	22111111	247	7	10	3211111
203	7	10	2221111	248	5	10	33211
204	7	10	2221111	249	6	12	222222
205	8	10	22111111	250	6	12	222222
206	8	10	22111111	251	6	10	322111
207	8	10	31111111	252	6	10	322111
208	7	10	3211111	253	7	10	3211111
209	8	10	22111111	254	7	10	2221111
210	6	10	322111	255	8	10	22111111
211	8	10	22111111	256	6	10	222211
212	8	10	22111111	257	7	10	3211111
213	8	10	22111111	258	9	10	211111111
214	7	10	3211111	259	9	10	211111111
215	7	10	3211111	260	9	10	211111111
216	9	10	211111111	261	9	10	211111111
217	10	10	1111111111	262	10	10	1111111111
218	8	10	22111111	263	9	10	211111111
219	10	10	1111111111	264	9	10	211111111
220	9	10	211111111	265	9	10	211111111
221	10	10	1111111111	266	9	10	211111111
222	9	10	211111111	267	9	10	211111111
223	10	10	1111111111	268	9	10	211111111
224	10	10	1111111111	269	10	10	1111111111
225	7	10	2221111	270	9	10	211111111

Epoch	Groups	Indi-viduals	Sizes of groups	Epoch	Groups	Indi-viduals	Sizes of groups
271	10	10	1111111111	< 316	5	10	33211
272	9	10	211111111	317	9	10	211111111
273	9	10	211111111	318	6	10	222211
274	10	10	1111111111	319	6	10	222211
275	10	10	1111111111	320	8	10	22111111
276	10	10	1111111111	321	9	10	211111111
277	8	10	22111111	322	9	10	211111111
278	7	10	2221111	323	6	10	222211
279	8	10	22111111	324	7	10	3211111
< 280	5	10	32221	325	8	10	22111111
281	10	10	1111111111	326	10	10	1111111111
282	8	10	22111111	327	9	10	211111111
283	8	10	22111111	< 328	8	10	31111111
284	9	10	211111111	329	10	10	1111111111
285	8	10	22111111	330	10	10	1111111111
286	4	10	3322	331	10	10	1111111111
287	4	10	3331	332	9	10	211111111
288	5	10	33211	333	9	10	211111111
289	4	10	3322	334	9	10	211111111
290	5	10	33211	335	7	10	2221111
291	5	10	33211	336	9	10	211111111
< 292	6	10	421111	337	10	10	1111111111
293	9	10	211111111	338	10	10	1111111111
294	8	10	22111111	339	8	10	22111111
295	7	10	2221111	340	8	10	22111111
296	7	10	2221111	341	8	10	22111111
297	7	10	3211111	342	5	10	32221
298	5	10	32221	343	9	10	211111111
299	5	13	43222	344	8	10	22111111
300	4	10	3331	345	6	10	322111
< 301	5	10	42211	346	5	10	32221
302	8	10	22111111	347	6	15	432222
303	9	10	211111111	348	5	12	42222
304	10	10	1111111111	349	4	10	3322
305	9	10	211111111	350	5	10	33211
306	10	10	1111111111	351	5	12	33222
307	8	10	22111111	352	7	18	4332222
308	10	10	1111111111	353	6	16	333322
309	10	10	1111111111	354	6	15	333322
310	10	10	1111111111	< 355	9	10	211111111
311	8	10	22111111	356	9	10	211111111
312	9	10	211111111	357	8	10	31111111
313	5	10	32221	358	6	10	222211
314	7	10	3211111	359	8	10	22111111
315	5	10	32221	360	6	10	322111

Epoch	Groups	Indi-viduals	Sizes of groups	Epoch	Groups	Indi-viduals	Sizes of groups
361	8	10	31111111	406	8	10	22111111
362	6	10	322111	407	8	10	22111111
363	9	10	211111111	408	8	10	22111111
364	9	10	211111111	409	8	10	22111111
365	9	10	211111111	410	9	10	211111111
366	10	10	1111111111	411	10	10	1111111111
367	8	10	22111111	412	9	10	211111111
368	10	10	1111111111	413	10	10	1111111111
369	10	10	1111111111	414	8	10	22111111
370	10	10	1111111111	415	9	10	211111111
371	9	10	211111111	416	10	10	1111111111
372	9	10	211111111	417	9	10	211111111
373	9	10	211111111	418	9	10	211111111
374	10	10	1111111111	419	7	10	2221111
375	9	10	211111111	420	7	10	3211111
376	10	10	1111111111	421	8	10	22111111
377	10	10	1111111111	422	10	10	1111111111
378	10	10	1111111111	423	10	10	1111111111
379	9	10	211111111	424	9	10	211111111
380	9	10	211111111	425	10	10	1111111111
381	7	10	3211111	426	6	10	222211
382	8	10	31111111	427	6	10	331111
383	10	10	1111111111	428	7	18	4332222
384	10	10	1111111111	429	4	10	4222
385	10	10	1111111111	430	8	10	31111111
386	7	10	2221111	431	7	10	2221111
387	6	10	222211	432	8	10	22111111
388	6	10	222211	433	8	10	22111111
389	8	10	22111111	434	6	10	322111
390	9	10	211111111	435	9	10	211111111
391	9	10	211111111	436	9	10	211111111
392	6	10	322111	437	10	10	1111111111
393	6	10	322111	438	8	10	22111111
394	9	10	211111111	439	8	10	22111111
395	9	10	211111111	440	8	10	22111111
396	9	10	211111111	441	9	10	211111111
397	6	10	322111	442	8	10	22111111
398	7	10	3211111	443	8	10	22111111
399	6	10	322111	444	8	10	22111111
400	7	10	3211111	445	8	10	22111111
401	9	10	211111111	446	7	10	2221111
402	9	10	211111111	447	6	10	222211
403	8	10	22111111	448	6	10	222211
404	7	10	2221111	449	6	10	222211
405	5	10	32221	450	8	10	22111111

Table B5.4 (Continued)

Epoch	Groups	Individuals	Sizes of groups	Epoch	Groups	Individuals	Sizes of groups
451	10	10	1111111111	496	9	10	211111111
452	9	10	211111111	497	10	10	1111111111
453	10	10	1111111111	498	10	10	1111111111
454	9	10	211111111	499	9	10	211111111
455	10	10	1111111111	500	9	10	211111111
456	9	10	211111111	501	7	10	2221111
457	9	10	211111111	502	7	10	2221111
458	9	10	211111111	503	9	10	211111111
459	9	10	211111111	504	9	10	211111111
460	9	10	211111111	505	7	10	2221111
461	10	10	1111111111	506	8	10	22111111
462	9	10	211111111	507	8	10	22111111
463	10	10	1111111111	508	7	10	2221111
464	9	10	211111111	509	5	12	33222
465	8	10	22111111	< 510	4	10	3322
466	10	10	1111111111	511	8	10	31111111
467	9	10	211111111	512	5	10	32221
< 468	8	10	31111111	513	7	10	3211111
469	10	10	1111111111	514	6	10	331111
470	10	10	1111111111	< 515	6	10	421111
471	7	10	2221111	516	9	10	211111111
472	10	10	1111111111	517	10	10	1111111111
473	10	10	1111111111	518	10	10	1111111111
474	10	10	1111111111	519	10	10	1111111111
475	10	10	1111111111	520	9	10	211111111
476	10	10	1111111111	521	8	10	22111111
477	7	10	2221111	522	8	10	31111111
478	9	10	211111111	523	7	10	4111111
479	9	10	211111111	< 524	5	10	43111
480	8	10	22111111	< 525	4	13	4333
481	9	10	211111111	< 526	7	10	3211111
482	9	10	211111111	527	7	10	2221111
483	9	10	211111111	528	7	10	2221111
484	6	10	322111	529	5	11	32222
485	8	10	22111111	530	7	10	2221111
486	9	10	211111111	531	8	10	22111111
487	9	10	211111111	532	7	10	3211111
488	9	10	211111111	533	7	10	2221111
489	10	10	1111111111	534	6	10	222211
490	10	10	1111111111	535	7	10	2221111
491	7	10	2221111	536	5	10	32221
492	7	10	2221111	537	4	11	4322
493	6	10	222211	< 538	6	10	421111
494	7	10	2221111	< 539	3	10	433
495	10	10	1111111111	< 540	10	10	1111111111

Epoch	Groups	Indi-viduals	Sizes of groups	Epoch	Groups	Indi-viduals	Sizes of groups
541	9	10	211111111	571	8	10	22111111
542	7	10	2221111	572	4	10	3322
543	4	10	3322	573	5	10	32221
544	9	10	211111111	574	5	10	32221
545	8	10	22111111	575	8	10	22111111
546	9	10	211111111	576	7	10	2221111
547	10	10	1111111111	577	7	10	2221111
548	7	10	2221111	578	9	10	211111111
549	8	10	22111111	579	10	10	1111111111
550	8	10	22111111	580	9	10	211111111
551	7	10	2221111	581	8	10	22111111
552	9	10	211111111	582	9	10	211111111
553	10	10	1111111111	583	9	10	211111111
554	9	10	211111111	584	6	10	322111
555	9	10	211111111	585	6	10	322111
556	8	10	22111111	586	8	10	22111111
557	6	10	222211	587	9	10	211111111
558	9	10	211111111	588	9	10	211111111
559	8	10	22111111	589	9	10	211111111
560	6	10	222211	590	9	10	211111111
561	6	10	322111	591	9	10	211111111
562	6	10	322111	592	10	10	1111111111
563	5	10	32221	593	10	10	1111111111
564	5	10	32221	594	10	10	1111111111
565	7	10	3211111	595	9	10	211111111
566	8	10	31111111	596	10	10	1111111111
567	7	10	2221111	597	9	10	211111111
568	8	10	31111111	598	10	10	1111111111
569	8	10	31111111	599	10	10	1111111111
570	9	10	211111111	600	10	10	1111111111

6
Other
Relevant
Data

To extend the scope of the LOST models to a nontrivial range of social situations, this chapter examines the three distributions of human group sizes from James's data that Coleman's (1964) model could not account for. It also investigates four previously unanalyzed frequency distributions of sleeping group sizes of East African monkeys (Lumsden 1951) and the frequency distribution of the number of occupants in passenger cars in Los Angeles observed by Haight (1960). An alternative model for group formation proposed by Haight is also briefly considered. Finally, the failures of the LOST models in analyzing variable and mixed traffic flows and alliances of war are shown to have a reasonable relation to the models' specific assumptions.

6.1 James: The Discrepant Human Data

Coleman (1964:368–373) presents 21 frequency distributions of group size observed by James. Coleman remarks that only 3 of them fail to be well fitted by the truncated Poisson distribution. Table 6.1 reproduces those 3 distributions: set 4 (pedestrians); set 11 (play groups, public playground); and set 16 (public gatherings, public beach swimming pool).

Next to distributions 4 and 11 are fitted truncated negative binomial distributions. These good fits show that the models presented here can extend the range of human data amenable to efficient explanation.

Distribution 16 fails to meet Sampford's criterion (A2.8). Estimation of parameters by Brass's method leads to a negative value for r and a value of p greater than 1, which are clearly nonsense. To see whether the distribution could be accounted for by the generalized negative binomial distribution (4.10) with c possibly nonzero, Katz's (1945)

method of moments was applied to the distribution. First,
an asymptotic test of the hypothesis that $b = 0$ was per-
formed (Katz 1945:57). The test consisted in seeing whether
$s^2 - \hat{\mu}_3$ falls within the following 99 percent confidence
interval, where $\hat{\mu}_3$ is the estimate of the third central moment and T is the total number of observations:

$$\frac{2s^2}{T} \pm \frac{2(2.57)}{T^{1/2}} \left(2 + \frac{3s^2}{2} \right)^{1/2}. \tag{6.1}$$

(A factor of $2^{1/2}$ is missing from the second term in Katz
1945:57, who gives the full derivation.) Since, in this case,
$s^2 - \hat{\mu}_3$ fell within the interval given by (6.1), b was taken
as zero. The values of a and c were then estimated, following Katz, from

$$a = c = \frac{2(s^2)^2}{\hat{\mu}_3 + s^2}. \tag{6.2}$$

If b had not been taken as zero, it would have been estimated from

$$b = \frac{\hat{\mu}_3 - s^2}{\hat{\mu}_3 + s^2}. \tag{6.3}$$

The fit to distribution 16 in Table 6.1 is poor and the estimate of c is negative, hence the model simply does not
work for this situation. The excess of couples observed
relative to the number predicted may seem intuitively to
be related to the source of the observations: the beach of a
public swimming pool (where people have been known
to go for the purpose of forming couples). A model due to
Haight (see Section 6.3) offers a possibility of describing
even this phenomenon.

6.2 Lumsden: More Monkey Sleeping Groups

In studying the epidemiology of sylvan yellow fever in
a forest in Uganda, Lumsden (1951) selected 51 trees in
which monkeys of various species had been seen to sleep.
He had African assistants record the number of monkeys
of each species seen sleeping in each of those trees over a
six-month period. Of the eight species in his table (Lums-

Table 6.1. Three Recalcitrant Frequency Distributions of Sizes of Human Groups

Set	Group size	Observed frequency	Predicted frequency	Truncated negative binomial
4	1	1677	1677.5	$p = 0.854$
	2	331	330.7	$r = 1.701$
	3	59	59.6	$a = 0.248$
	4	12	10.2	$b = 0.146$
	$\geqslant 5$	1	2.0	$x^2 = 0.840$
				df = 2
11	1	316	318.7	$p = 0.716$
	2	106	96.1	$r = 1.127$
	3	19	28.4	$a = 0.320$
	4	10	8.3	$b = 0.284$
	5	$4\begin{cases}1\end{cases}$	$3.4\begin{cases}2.4\end{cases}$	$x^2 = 4.602$
	$\geqslant 6$	$\phantom{4\{}3$	$\phantom{3.4\{}.98$	df = 2
				Poisson arbitrary origin
16	1	276	302.0	$a = 0.612$
	2	229	199.8	$b = 0$
	3	61	63.5	$c = -0.075$
	4	12	13.3	$x^2 = 6.915$
	$\geqslant 5$	3	2.4	df = 2

Data are from Coleman (1964: 368-373). This table reports only three of the distributions James observed in Oregon: Set 4, pedestrians on a spring morning in Portland; set 11, play groups at public playground C in the spring in Eugene; set 16, public gatherings at a public beach swimming pool in the spring in Portland.

den 1951:24) of the distribution of sleeping group size, four species had frequencies totaling more than 50.

The four frequency distributions are given in Table 6.2. Application of the truncated Poisson variance test (1.4) to each distribution showed that the mean and variance of each could have come from a truncated Poisson distribution; the observations were not overdispersed. The truncated Poisson distributions fitted to each set of observations are also listed in Table 6.2.

According to the χ^2 test for goodness of fit, for two of the four species the probability is less than 0.01 that a random sample from the theoretical distribution would differ from it more than the observed. The fit for the other two species is acceptable, but it should be noted that these two species have the smaller sample sizes.

Lumsden noted that the "bands" (troops, as used here) of these four species seen in the daytime usually numbered over 10 individuals, and he suggests that these larger troops may break up at evening into smaller sleeping groups, exactly as Struhsaker observed. But instead

Table 6.2. Observed and Fitted Truncated Poisson Frequency Distributions of Sleeping Group Size in Four Species of Ugandan Forest Monkeys[a]

Group size	Cercocebus albigena johnstoni Observ.	Cercocebus albigena johnstoni Pred.	Cercocebus ascanius schmidti Observ.	Cercocebus ascanius schmidti Pred.	Papio doguera tessellatus Observ.	Papio doguera tessellatus Pred.	Colobus abyssinicus ituricus Observ.	Colobus abyssinicus ituricus Pred.
1	4	11.5	0	3.3	11	9.9	41	18.9
2	17	24.7	8	7.9	18	21.7	26	36.8
3	44	35.3	11	12.5	22	31.5	24	47.8
4	53	37.8	25	14.9	53	34.5	42	46.6
5	28	32.5	12	14.3	30	30.1	36	36.3
6	33	23.2	11	11.3	17	21.9	48	23.6
7	6	14.2	5	7.7	10	13.7	11	13.2
8	4	7.6	5	4.6	10	7.5	2	6.4
9	1	3.6	2	2.4	3	3.6	2	2.8
10	0	1.6	1	1.2	3	2.6	2	1.6
11	0	0.6	0	0.5	—	—	—	—
12	2	2.5 { 0.2	1	2.0 { 0.3	—	—	—	—
13	1	0.1	—	—	—	—	—	—
Total	193		81		177		234	
λ	4.29		4.77		4.37		3.90	
x^2	28.74		11.70		16.74		70.30	
df	8		8		8		8	
$p <$	0.01		0.20		0.05		0.01	

Data from Lumsden (1951:24).

[a]Predicted frequency for the highest observed group size of each species includes the tail of the distribution; thus, for C. a. ituricus the predicted frequency of a group of size ≥ 10 is 1.6.

of following the members of a given troop, as Struhsaker did, Lumsden observed given trees. Since monkeys of the species *Colobus abyssinicus ituricus*, and especially solitary monkeys of this species, preferred particular sleeping trees, this difference in procedure may have affected all four of the observed distributions. For example, noting that only in the species *C. a. ituricus* were solitary monkeys very frequent, Lumsden comments (1951:23):

Such a result does not necessarily imply that solitary monkeys were not of common occurrence in the species other than *C. a. ituricus*, but only that if they occurred they tended not to use the study trees for sleeping. Solitary *C. a. ituricus* occurred in eleven trees, all of which were also used from time to time by bands, but four trees, numbers 41, 44, 48 and 51, accounted for thirty-two out of the forty-one observations. Tree no. 51 was especially used; eleven out of the thirteen times it was occupied were by solitary monkeys.

Since the trees were intentionally selected from the forest not at random but as trees where observers had seen sleeping groups of monkeys and since larger groups were more likely to be seen in trees than small ones, the selection of trees was biased against those used idiosyncratically by isolates or by small groups. In view of this bias, and the possible unreliability of the method of gathering data, a fit to or failure to fit the truncated Poisson distribution cannot be taken too seriously.

6.3 Haight: Passenger Car Occupancy

Haight (1960) observed the occupancy of more than 14,000 vehicles on the roads around Los Angeles. His prime set of data (1960:14, sample number 6.7) is the distribution of occupancy in 1469 passenger cars observed passing a fixed spot within one hour's time. The virtues of this set of data are that the vehicles included are homogeneous, or nearly so, in their capacity and that the time period spanned is short.

The truncated Poisson variance test showed that the distribution of occupancy was overdispersed. Therefore, next to the observed frequencies in Table 6.3 are the fitted frequencies of a truncated negative binomial distribution. Other Relevant Data

Table 6.3. Frequency Distribution of Occupancy of Passenger Cars in Los Angeles and Two Predicted Distributions

Group size	Observed frequency	Truncated negative binomial	Haight
1	902	906.2	898.2
2	403	380.2	407.1
3	106	129.3	109.7
4	38	38.8	37.4
5	16	10.7	11.4
$\geqslant 6$	4	3.7	5.3
		$p = 0.819$	$\beta = 0.224$
		$r = 3.629$	$\rho = 0.212$
		$X^2 = 8.201$	$X^2 = 2.408$
		df = 3	df = 3
		$0.02 < P < 0.05$	$0.3 < P < 0.5$

Data from Haight (1960: Sample 6.7).

Since X^2 is not too large, and since each new vehicle is an independent observation, the assumption that the observations were drawn from a truncated negative binomial distribution cannot be rejected.

Admittedly, there is little superficial similarity between groups of four-year-olds at play in Cambridge Nursery School and the occupants of passenger cars on Wilshire Boulevard at Bundy Drive in Los Angeles, where Haight made these observations. Access to a group of occupants in an automobile is difficult (as hitchhikers know), and spontaneous departure from an occupant group in that stream of traffic could be perilous. While the automobiles may have picked up or discharged passengers en route, Haight has no information on the magnitudes of these two opposite effects, nor have we.

The similarity of these occupant groups to monkeys asleep in East African treetops is not so remote, however. In both cases, a cluster of individuals is frozen together during the period of observation; among Struh-saker's vervets, membership in a sleeping group was fixed, on peril of death, during the night. In the cases of both the vervets and the passenger car occupants, it is plausible, I argue, to assume that the period of fixed group membership is preceded and followed by free mixing of the sort described by the LOST models. James's data, showing that the distributions of pedestrian group sizes and of shopping group sizes follow the truncated Poisson or truncated negative binomial, support the assumption that the groups of occupants could have been sampled from unconstrained pedestrian or shopping groups.

While it may be objected that occupant groups of automobiles cannot be freely forming because automobile capacities truncate the upper tail of any size distribution, it should be noted (Table 6.3) that the upper tail observed is not pushing against the capacity of most automobiles (6 passengers) and that the frequency of groups of size 5, 6, or larger is very low even among unconstrained pedestrian and play groups. Limited automobile capacity would not seem to affect importantly the distribution of occupant group size, as long as these are "interacting" groups (that is, excluding buses).

Proof that the LOST models apply to these occupant groups must await data on what happens to the groups before and after their trips down Wilshire Boulevard. In the meantime, on the basis of a plausibility argument, the agreement of Haight's observations with the truncated negative binomial distribution will be taken as an extension of the scope of the LOST models.

Also included in Table 6.3 is a fit of the data to a distribution proposed by Haight to account for the finding that, in many of his samples, fits of several classical distributions predicted too few couples in comparison to the number observed. Haight proposed the following theory of "three's a crowd." Consider occupants of automobiles to be of two types, men and women. Suppose the probability that there are exactly $n = 1, 2, \ldots$, men in a car is q_n. Suppose also that for each man in a car, there is a probability β that he is accompanied by a woman and probability $1 - \beta$ that he is not accompanied by a woman. If p_n is the probability that there are exactly n occupants in a car, regardless of sex, then clearly $p_1 = Pr$ (one man without a woman) $= q_1(1 - \beta)$, $p_2 = Pr$ (two men without women) $+ Pr$ (one man with woman) $= q_2(1 - \beta)^2 + q_1\beta$, and in general

$$p_n = \sum_{i=0}^{[n/2]} \binom{n-i}{i} q_{n-i}(1 - \beta)^{n-2i}\beta^i, \qquad (6.4)$$

where $[x]$ is the greatest integer less than or equal to x. Haight (1960:7, 1967:53) credits Hirata (1933) and Terao (1949) with the independent invention of this distribution.

Since the geometric distribution with origin at 1, given by

$$q_n = (1 - \rho)\rho^{n-1}, \qquad n = 1, 2, \ldots, 0 < \rho < 1, \quad (6.5)$$

had given the best description of occupancy of those single parameter distributions that Haight considered, he adopted it for the $\{q_n\}$. This choice may be defended either as an irreducibly simple model that says that the arrivals of successive men to a car are independent and of fixed probability or as the special case of the negative binomial distribution with origin at 1 in which the parameter r equals 1. Then if $\bar{x}$ is the calculated mean occupancy of the observed distribution and if s^2 is the calculated variance, Haight shows that the parameters β and ρ should satisfy

$$\bar{x} = \frac{1 + \beta}{1 - \rho} \qquad (6.6)$$

and

$$s^2 + (\bar{x})^2 - \bar{x} = \frac{2\beta}{1 - \rho} + \frac{2\rho(1 + \beta)^2}{(1 - \rho)^2}. \qquad (6.7)$$

[He gives (6.7) with a mistake in sign.] Hence β is a root of

$$2\bar{x}\beta^2 + (s^2 - (\bar{x})^2 + \bar{x})\beta + (s^2 - (\bar{x})^2 + \bar{x}) = 0, \qquad (6.8)$$

and ρ may then be found from (6.6). With these parameters in hand, the probabilities (6.4) may be more easily calculated from the recursion relation

$$p_n = \rho[(1 - \beta)p_{n-1} + \beta p_{n-2}], \qquad n = 3, 4, \ldots. \quad (6.9)$$

I recalculated the parameters and predicted frequencies of the Haight distribution for Haight's data, as shown in Table 6.3, and found the fit substantially better than that obtained by Haight himself (1960:8), who calculated the parameters to lesser accuracy. As is obvious in Table 6.3, the fit is also superior to that of the truncated negative binomial distribution.

To find out the generality of the Haight distribution, I chose arbitrarily another of Haight's samples, number 4.14, which consisted of 2189 vehicles of all kinds observed within 70 minutes at one corner. The data are given in Table 6.4. The equation (6.8) for β had only imaginary roots.

Table 6.4 Distribution of Occupancy of Vehicles at a Los Angeles Corner[a]

Group size	Observed	Truncated negative binomial
1	1465	1473.3
2	522	478.3
3	120	158.1
4	51	52.7
5	10	17.7
$\geqslant 6$	21	9.0
		$p = 0.658$
		$r = 0.898$
		$x^2 = 32.742$
		$df = 3$
		$P < 0.001$

Data from Haight (1960: Sample 4.14).
[a]All north and southbound vehicles were observed at the corner of LaCienega and Beverly Blvds., Los Angeles.

Since the chief problem with Coleman's set 16 (public beach swimming pool) was the excess of couples, the Haight distribution was fitted to those data (Table 6.5): the fit is substantially poorer than that of the two-parameter Poisson distribution with arbitrary origin (Table 6.1) and would be rejected by the χ^2 test.

For all four of Lumsden's sets of observations, the roots of (6.8) fell outside the interval [0, 1] and thus could not be interpreted as the probability β.

Struhsaker's vervet data give a root $\beta = 0.76$. The predicted distribution that results is compared with the observed distribution in Table 6.6. A nice feature of these

Table 6.5. Fit of the Haight Distribution to Coleman's Set 16[a]

Group size	Observed frequency	Haight
1	276	261.3
2	229	267.9
3	61	30.6
4	12	17.0
≥ 5	3	4.2

$$\beta = 0.491$$
$$\rho = 0.116$$
$$x^2 = 38.403$$
$$df = 2$$

[a]See Table 6.1.

Table 6.6. Fits of the Haight Distribution to Struhsaker's Data

Group size	Obs. freq.	Haight Fit 1[a]	Haight Fit 2	Obs. freq.	Haight Fit 3	Haight Fit 4
1	19	9.6	22.3	27	36.0	33.2
2	14	32.0	17.5	29	28.3	28.0
3	19	8.3	13.0	24	20.9	20.6
4	11	14.7	9.7	20	15.7	15.8
5	7	5.5	7.2	12	11.7	11.9
6	7	7.0	5.4	9	8.7	9.1
7	3	3.2	4.0	5	6.5	6.9
8	2	3.4	3.0	4	4.9	5.2
9	3	1.8	2.2	9	3.6	4.0
10	1	1.7	1.7	2	2.7	3.0
11	2	1.8 { 1.0	1.3	2	2.0	2.3
12	0	{ 0.8	1.6 { 0.9	0	1.5	1.7
13	1	2.0 { 0.5	{ 0.7	1	1.1	1.3
≥14	2	{ 1.5	2.1	2	1.5 { 0.8	1.7 { 1.0
15	—	—	—	0	{ 0.6	{ 0.8
16	—	—	—	0	1.9 { 0.5	2.4 { 0.6
≥17	—	—	—	1	{ 1.4	{ 1.8

		$\beta = 0.763$	$\beta = 0.165$		$\beta = 0.165$	$\beta = 0.230$
		$\rho = 0.557$	$\rho = 0.707$		$\rho = 0.707$	$\rho = 0.707$
		$x^2 = 36.685$	$x^2 = 6.493$		$x^2 = 14.662$	$x^2 = 13.098$
		$df = 9$	$df = 10$		$df = 12$	$d\tau = 12$
		$P < 0.001$	$0.7 < P < 0.8$		$0.2 < P < 0.3$	$0.3 < P < 0.5$

[a]Fit 1 parameters satisfy equations (6.6) and (6.8); parameters of other fits do not.

predictions is that they are bimodal, as are the observations. Unfortunately, the predicted ups and downs do not coincide with the observed, and the fit would be rejected by the χ^2 test. However, taking another parameter value (discovered by accident) yields a predicted Haight distribution that, while monotonic, is in excellent agreement with Struhsaker's observations, according to the χ^2 test (Table 6.6).

This example makes it uncertain whether the failures of the Haight distribution are due to an inadequate estimation procedure or to the distribution itself. Several trials of other parameter values with the other observed distributions did not result in startling improvements. Hence, for the time being, the truncated negative binomial distribution is still to be preferred to the Haight distribution on the grounds of its generality. Questions of fit aside, the Haight model also does not pertain to systems of groups in the "sociological" sense defined by Goodman (1964), since it views each group as an independent replicate of the same process. Such a viewpoint, while possibly reasonable for automobile occupancy, is clearly insufficient for the situation of the vervet monkeys.

6.4 Do the LOST Models Fail Appropriately?

The LOST models proposed in Chapter 4 are useful only if they can serve as a guide to deciding when to expect a truncated negative binomial distribution of group sizes and when not. Failing such guidance, it could only be concluded that the distributions fitting the truncated negative binomial arose accidentally from a much larger and poorly understood universe of systems of groups. The purpose of this section is to cite examples of situations in which the processes by which groups are formed seem clearly not to satisfy the assumptions of the LOST models, open or closed, and which therefore cannot be expected to conform to the predictions of those models.

In the first situation, Haight (1960: sample 4.14) observed the occupancy of "all north- and southbound vehicles" in 5-minute samples out of every 10 minutes from 1:40 to 2:50 P.M. on the corner of two major traffic arteries in Los Angeles. Since this sample comprised motorcycles, passenger automobiles, trucks, and busses, the rates of arrival a and b or of departure d could not be independent of group size and constant throughout the sample: busses can hold far more than cars or motorcycles. Table 6.4 shows that the fit of the observed distribution to the truncated negative binomial distribution is poor.

In the second situation, Haight (1960: sample 9.41), observed only passenger cars in 5-minute samples every half hour over a 20-hour period, starting at 5:30 A.M. one morning and ending at 1:30 A.M. the following morning. Here the capacities of the vehicles are constant or nearly so. But since the mean vehicle occupancy (size of group) fluctuated from 1.23 in an early-morning sample to 2.34 in a late-evening sample, it cannot be presumed that the coefficients a, b, and d defining the equilibrium distribution were constant. Hence, the total distribution cannot be expected to be a truncated negative binomial. Table 6.7 confirms that the observations are poorly described by a truncated negative binomial distribution.

If this (here unexplained) variability in the parameter

Table 6.7. Distribution of Occupancy in a 20-Hour Sample of Passenger Cars in Los Angeles[a]

Group size	Observed	Truncated negative binomial
1	1372	1400.9
2	934	796.3
3	207	337.3
4	123	118.4
5	41	36.4
$\geqslant$ 6	26	13.6
		$p = 0.866$
		$r = 7.496$
		$x^2 = 86.793$
		df = 3
		$P < 0.001$

Data from Haight (1960: sample 9.41).
[a]East-bound passenger cars only on Wilshire Blvd. at Wellesley Ave.

values is responsible for the failure of the open LOST model, then less variable subsamples of Haight's observation ought to come closer to expectations. Table 6.8 gives Haight's sample 9.41 broken down into three blocks: (1) observations from 5:30 A.M. to 12 noon (his samples 9.1–9.13); (2) from 12 noon to 6 P.M. (samples 9.14–9.25); and (3) from 6 P.M. to 1:30 A.M. (samples 9.26–9.40). In the first block, the range of mean occupancy among the half-hour samples was 0.32 (from 1.23 to 1.55); in the second, the range was 0.50 (from 1.42 to 1.92); and in the third, the range was 0.63 (from 1.71 to 2.34). If variability in parameters causes disagreement with the LOST model, the first block should agree best with the truncated negative binomial distribution, since it has the smallest range of mean occupancy per 5-minute subsample, and the third block should agree worst.

Table 6.8. Distribution of Occupancy of Passenger Cars During Three Time Intervals

Group size	Observed 5:30 a.m. to 12 noon	Truncated negative binomial	Observed 12 noon to 6 p.m.	Truncated negative binomial	Observed 6 p.m. to 1:30 a.m.
1	521	522.2	551	555.9	300
2	165	157.1	275	245.0	494
3	35	45.2	66	97.0	106
4	16	12.7	33	36.2	74
5	3	3.5	20	13.0	18
$\geqslant 6$	2	1.3	9	4.6	15

$$p = 0.738 \qquad p = 0.694$$
$$r = 1.301 \qquad r = 1.881$$
$$x^2 = 3.973 \qquad x^2 = 18.229$$
$$df = 3 \qquad df = 3$$
$$0.2 < P < 0.3 \qquad P < 0.001$$

Data from Haight (1960: sample 9).

Table 6.8 shows that the first block is acceptably fitted by the truncated negative binomial distribution. The fit to the second block is poor, although the moments satisfy Sampford's (1955) criterion. The moments of the third block do not even satisfy that criterion, and estimation of the parameters by the method of Brass leads to nonsense values. (In this third block, the high average occupancy also means that the truncation of group sizes above 6, because of the limited capacity of automobiles, is more likely to render impossible the assumed constancy of rates of arrival for all group sizes.)

Aside from systems of freely forming groups like these two examples, there are many more institutionalized social situations in which the LOST models must fail: for example, at a formal dance with couples only or on a playground with organized group play (see Section 8.1 for examples). Both these institutionalized situations and the two situations observed by Haight fail to satisfy the assumptions of not only the LOST models, but of any of a broad class of models that assume at least stable average parameters and homogeneous samples. Hence, the failure to predict the group size distribution in such situations does not confirm the detailed form of the equations of the LOST models, but only the necessity of the more general assumptions.

Horvath and Foster (1963) studied a third situation—the formation of alliances among nations for war—that could be assumed to have stable average parameters and the sample of which included all known cases. This situation differs in at least two respects from the situation of Coleman and James: the individuals involved are nations, not people; and the groups are formed for aggressive, not fraternal, purposes.

Horvath and Foster found that the distribution of size of alliance was described not by the truncated negative binomial or Poisson distributions but by another, called the Yule distribution. The Yule distribution "postulates that nations join alliances of a given size at a rate proportional to the total number of nations in alliances of that size and that alliances break up into their constituent members at a constant rate independent of size" (Horvath and Foster 1963:116). Thus, the joining of groups proceeds as in the LOST models with parameter a equal to zero and b positive. But, unlike the informal groups of Coleman and James that are merely reduced in size when one

131

member departs, "no member leaves an aggressive group until the whole group is dissolved" (Horvath and Foster 1963:116).

It remains to be seen whether the kinetics of groups of friendly nations (in cooperating committees of the United Nations, for example) would be described by the LOST models, and whether the kinetics of groups of aggressive people (terrorist bands or criminal gangs) would be characterized by the Yule distribution. If either aggregation for aggression or the nature of the aggregating individuals alter social kinetics, then the failure of the LOST models to describe the size distribution of alliances for war is to be expected.

While finding that the LOST models fail when they ought to makes them more useful, such a finding does not show the truth of the detailed social process they assume. In the situations considered in this chapter, that proof depends on observations yet unmade.

7
Individual
Behavior,
Social
Organization,
and
Population
Ecology

So far, the level of analysis has been exclusively social. The identities of individuals have been caricatured by averages sufficient for those residual situations in which no imposed organization was detected. Influences of the environment on social groups, and influences of social groups on the responses of individuals to their environment, have been ignored up to now. This chapter reports three attempts to bind the present social study into an understanding of individuals belonging to species situated in environments.

7.1 Social Data Reveal Individual Differences

If Struhsaker had observed only the size of sleeping groups on each night, it would be possible to show only that the frequency of isolates in a block of observations of group size is distributed binomially, as expected. However, because Struhsaker also recorded the identity of the animals in each group, finer analysis is possible. We will now show that the animals are not equally exposed to isolation.

Independently of the preceding models, let p_i be the probability of a group of size i, $i = 1, 2, \ldots$, and suppose that the group sizes observed are a random sample from some probability distribution $\{p_i\}_{i=1}^{\infty}$. The following results do not depend on whether the $\{p_i\}$ specify a negative binomial or any other particular distribution.

Define the indicator variable N_{1j} by $N_{1j} = 1$ if a group labeled j is of size 1 (with probability p_1) and $N_{1j} = 0$ otherwise (with probability $1 - p_1$). In a block of B observations (assumed to be a random sample of size B), the number of isolates, or the number of groups of size 1, is $N_{11} + \cdots + N_{1B}$; since each N_{1j} is Bernoulli distributed, the sum has the binomial distribution with mean Bp_1 and variance $Bp_1(1 - p_1)$.

133

(Katz 1952 also derives a binomial distribution for the frequency of isolates, but his definition of isolates and the way in which they arise are quite different. Hence, these are independent results.) The number of groups of size i in a block of B observations will similarly have a binomial distribution with mean Bp_i and variance $Bp_i(1-p_i)$. At present, only the distribution of isolates will be examined.

Since Struhsaker's list (Section 1.3) has 91 observations of sleeping group size, let $B = 10$. There are thus 9 blocks of B observations each. Table 7.1 records the frequency

Table 7.1. Frequency of Isolates Per Block of 10 Groups in Struhsaker's Vervet Troop

	Frequency	
Number of isolates	Groups as listed in Section 1.1	Randomly permuted
0	1	0
1	2	3
2	2	4
3	4	1
4	0	0
5	0	1
Total	9	9
	Mean = 2.000	Mean = 2.111
	Variance = 1.250	Variance = 1.611
	x^2 = 6.25	x^2 = 7.76
	df = 8	df = 8
	$0.5 < P < 0.7$	$0.3 < P < 0.5$

distribution of the number of isolates per block of 10 observations. Two ways of forming the blocks are included: first, by proceeding through Struhsaker's list sequentially and stopping every 10 groups; and second, by randomly permuting the order of the 91 groups and then taking every 10. When the blocks are taken sequentially, only 18 isolates are observed, because the last group in the list is an isolate. Under the random permutation, that last isolate is included, giving the full 19 recorded in Table 1.2.

Although 9 observations (of frequency of isolates per

block) are too few to justify fitting a full binomial frequency distribution, a variance test analogous to that used for the Poisson distribution may be applied (Cochran 1954). Since, in the binomial distribution, the mean times $(1 - p_1)$ equals the variance, asymptotically the expression

$$X^2 = \frac{(T-1)s^2}{q_1\bar{x}}, \qquad (7.1)$$

should have the distribution of χ^2 with df $= T - 1$. Here T is the number of blocks ($T = 9$). For the blocks made by taking the groups as listed, $q_1 = 1 - 18/90$; the randomly permuted series gives $q_1 = 1 - 19/90$. In neither case can the assumption of a binomial distribution of number of isolates per block of groups be rejected.

While isolation looks simple from the point of view of a system of groups, it looks considerably less so from the point of view of the individuals involved. Suppose each individual's chance of falling in a group of size i on a given night is proportional to ip_i, that is, to the probability of a group of size i times the number of places for him in it. This assumption would follow from treating individuals as indistinguishable (Section 3.2). Less restrictively, suppose simply that on each night all individuals have an equal probability of being an isolate. The probability of an individual's being an isolate on a night will in general be different from p_1. But if the probability has some constant value for all animals and from night to night, then the frequency distribution of the number of nights an animal spends in isolation should be binomially distributed, by an argument like the one above.

Table 7.2 gives the frequency distribution of the number of nights spent alone by animals that were present for all 22 nights of observation. Since animals II, XV, and XVI were not present for all 22 nights, the frequency distribution sums only to 14. In the first frequency distribution in Table 7.2, animals that were paired with one of II, XV, or XVI were not counted as being isolated on that night. In the second frequency distribution in that table, those 3 animals were ignored; that is, other animals paired with one of them were considered isolated for that night. In both cases, the variances of the frequency distributions are

Table 7.2. Frequency of Isolation for Each Vervet Monkey Present All 22 Days[a]

	Number of Animals	
Nights of isolation	Counting II, XV, XVI as company	Not counting II, XV, XVI as company
0	9	7
1	0	0
2	2	2
3	1	2
4	1	1
5	0	1
6	1	1
	$N = 14$	$N = 14$
	Mean $= 1.214$	Mean $= 1.786$
	Variance $= 3.566$	Variance $= 4.489$

[a]Excluding II, XV, and XVI.

greater than the respective means; hence, the distributions cannot be binomial. This conclusion is confirmed by calculating X^2 for each distribution. The assumption that all animals have an equal probability of isolation on a given night must be rejected.

Table 7.3 lists individually the 14 monkeys included in Table 7.2 and gives a brief characterization of each along with the number of nights of isolation (counting animals II, XV, XVI as "unmonkeys"). There is no clear correlation between frequency of isolation and age, sex, or social rank. Here, a more detailed theory of individual behavior is needed to explain, in terms of parameters characterizing individuals, what the social data clearly reveal to be individual differences. The existence of individual differences does not invalidate the use of average parameters. For example, it is as averages that the parameters a, b, c, and d of the LOST models in Chap. 4 must be interpreted. The fine structure of social behavior simply calls for more finely structured explanations.

Table 7.3. Number of Nights of Isolation and Mean and Variance of Size of Group in which Each Animal Occurred[a]

Animal	Description	Nights of isolation	Mean size of group	Variance
I	adult m.	3	5.77	14.18
II	older subadult m.		6.85	26.97
III	adult m.	6	4.14	11.55
IV	adult f.	0	6.91	15.42
V	juvenile m.	2	7.05	14.90
VI	adult f.	2	6.86	12.98
VII	young juvenile f.	0	7.23	11.61
VIII	young juvenile f.	0	7.36	11.10
IX	young juvenile f.	0	6.09	14.94
X	juvenile f.	3	5.73	15.54
XI	subadult f.	4	3.95	8.24
XII	adult f.	5	5.18	12.25
XIII	2 young juvenile m.	0	6.95	12.93
XIV	infant m.	0	7.18	14.25
XV	infant f.		5.62	15.65
XVI	infant m.		7.15	13.29

[a]Not counting II, XV, and XVI as company.

7.2 Genetic and Adaptive Implications of Groupings

In a fine analysis of the associations of female paper wasps founding new colonies, West (1967) revealed the genetic advantage of a dominance hierarchy not only to the most dominant egg-laying queen but also to her lower ranking nonreproductive siblings. Using the theory of Hamilton (1964), she hypothesized

that dominance relations during group formation may maximize [the ratio of gain to loss in fitness] for each individual by enhancing the likelihood that relatively inferior reproductives—females likely to have few progeny on their own—become workers on nests of superior reproductives [with similar genes], which are thus free to specialize in egg laying (West 1967:1584).

137

More generally,

dominance could function as suggested here in any social species having groups composed of genetically similar (related) individuals, and dominance hierarchies in which (i) dominance reflects reproductive capacity, (ii) dominant individuals are the primary reproductives, and (iii) the presence or activity of a subordinate augments the reproduction of the dominant. These conditions may exist in some primate societies (West 1967:1585).

Vervet monkey troops certainly satisfy all these conditions (Struhsaker 1967c), and West's hypothesis suggests very nicely the advantage of a dominance hierarchy to them, as troops.

West shows the role of the dominance hierarchy in the population. The problem here is to show the role of the formation of groups in the population. Given such a nice account of dominance as West's, it is reasonable to try to relate group formation to dominance and to go from there to the population level. The following two unsuccessful attempts to relate group formation to dominance suggest, however, that a different approach may be necessary.

The first attempt is to search for some kind of an exclusion principle, analogous to that employed in Fermi-Dirac statistics (Feller 1957:39). Perhaps two animals of adjacent ranks, or two animals of sufficiently different rank, cannot occur in the same group. However, any such principle is excluded by the observations that on one night all monkeys slept together. Even in the necessarily more intimate groups containing 6 animals or fewer, Struhsaker's tabulation (1967c:112) of the pair combinations that occurred reveals no apparent pattern in the excluded possibilities.

Stuart A. Altmann has pointed out (personal communication, 11 April 1968) that a weakened version of this approach would be to investigate the probabilities of pairs sleeping together as a function of the difference in dominance between them. Though this possibility has not been checked carefully, a nonrandom influence of dominance difference on pairing frequency is not immediately apparent from Struhsaker's tabulation (1967c:112).

A second approach to discovering a relation between dominance and group formation is to examine the frequency distribution of each individual's occurrence in groups of each size. Perhaps there is a tendency for more dominant animals to sleep in groups of smaller (or larger) size; or, perhaps, more dominant animals are more (or less) variable in the size of group with which they spend the night.

Table 7.3 presents the mean and variance of the size of groups in which each animal occurred. The animals are listed in order of dominance from most to least. There is no obvious relation between dominance rank and mean or variance.

Incidentally, to predict approximately the means and variances of these individual distributions, it is sufficient to assume that group sizes are negative binomially distributed with probabilities p_k,

$$p_k = \binom{r+k-1}{k} p^r q^k, \qquad k = 0, 1, 2, \ldots, \qquad (7.2)$$

and then to find the mean and variance of the distribution of the number of places available in groups of each size, that is, the mean and variance of the distribution with probabilities t_k proportional to kp_k. Since the t_k's must sum to one,

$$t_k = \left(\frac{p}{rq}\right) kp_k, \qquad k = 1, 2, \ldots. \qquad (7.3)$$

The mean of the truncated distribution (7.3) is given by

$$\frac{1 + rq}{p}, \qquad (7.4)$$

and its variance is

$$\frac{1 + q + rq}{p^2}. \qquad (7.5)$$

For the distribution in Table 1.2 ("complete" nights only), the estimated parameters are $p = 0.34$ and $r = 1.74$. Hence, the predicted mean size of group in which an animal is found (7.4) is 6.318 and the predicted variance (7.5) is 24.291. For all the vervet data (Table 1.3) the estimated parameters are $p = 0.35$ and $r = 1.92$, with predicted mean 6.423 and predicted variance 23.657. In Table 7.3, the median observed size of group is 6.86 and the median variance is 13.73. Thus, observed and predicted means agree well, and while most observed variances are smaller than that predicted, at least one variance is larger. Truncation of the theoretical distribution above 17 would bring the predicted variance closer to the median observed.

Dominance "behavior may be expressed in some aspects of life and not in others," according to Etkin (1964:17). The two preceding failures to discern the role of dominance suggest that among vervets the formation of groups may be one aspect of life where dominance is not expressed. Since heterosexual activity is very closely correlated with the expression of dominance and since sleeping groups form at night in trees, if dominance has little to do with these groups, then heterosexual activities should take place mostly during the day and on the ground. In fact they do (Struhsaker 1967b:26–27). Vervets use sleeping groups for sleeping.

The apparent irrelevance of social dominance to the formation of sleeping groups is surprising in view of the significance that Struhsaker (1967c:114–115) attaches to the groups:

The temporary separation of [troop] members, that occurs when sleeping [groups] are formed, provides a situation that could enhance the formation of new social [troops] . . . Monkeys of different sleeping [groups] might prolong their morning reunion more and more each day until eventually they no longer reunite and instead form two or more new and separate social [troops] . . . A gradual parting . . . would allow the monkeys to expand and explore new regions while maintaining a familiar area as a food source and refuge from predators.

If, as the evidence shows, dominance has little to do with the composition of sleeping groups, then some groups may completely lack dominant males who are good reproducers.

7.3 Noise: An Ecological Limit on Group Size

Individual
Behavior,
Social
Organization,
and
Population
Ecology

If the form of the distribution of group sizes can be understood as the outcome of some social process, the question of why the parameters of that process are what they are still remains. This section will propose an explanation of why, in James's 21 series of observations of freely forming small groups (Coleman 1964:368–373), the maximum size in 12 series was 5, and the maximum size in 9 series was 6 and why his average group sizes were between 1 and 2.

James (1951:474) counted only "groups in which the members were in face-to-face interaction as evidenced by the criteria of gesticulation, laughter, smiles, talk, play or work." If the possibility for every member of the group to talk to every other one is taken as the criterion for its existence, then the distance between members of the group cannot be greater than that over which speech is intelligible. That distance is limited by the background noise above which speech must be heard. Information on typical background noise levels in the situations in which James observed groups and on the effect of distance and background noise on speech intelligibility should make it possible to calculate the maximum possible distance between members of a group.

Assume that a typical group has the geometry of a regular polygon. The members of the group stand at the vertices of the polygon. Then the maximum possible distance between members of a group is the maximum possible diameter of the circle circumscribing the polygon. If it is also assumed that because of social convention there is a minimum distance between any two people in public conversation, hence a minimum length to each edge of the inscribed polygon, then not more than a certain number of vertices (people in the group) can be fitted into the circle. We now determine the maximum number of people per group as a function of background noise level and then estimate minimum noise levels, which permit maximum group sizes, in situations typical of those James observed.

Beranek (1954:420, table 13.8) tabulates speech interference levels (defined below) that barely permit reliable word intelligibility at given distances and voice levels

141

when two men face each other in an open noise field. Since the speech interference levels must be 5 decibels (dB) lower for women to speak intelligibly than for men, and since James's groups typically included women and children, the values in Table 7.4 are all 5 dB lower than Beranek's. Beranek's tabulation of speech interference levels is identical to (and probably the source of) that given by Hawley and Kryter (1957:11), who point out that these figures assume

Table 7.4. Speech Interference Levels Barely Permitting Reliable Word Intelligibility, Women Speaking (in dB re 0.0002 microbar)

Maximum distance L (feet)	Voice level		
	Normal	Raised	Very loud
0.5	66	72	78
1	60	66	72
2	54	60	66
3	50	56	62
4	48	54	60
5	46	52	58
6	44	50	56
12	38	44	50

Based on Beranek (1954: 420).

that the listener obtained no appreciable cues regarding the speech signal as the result of observing the facial, lip, and mouth movements of the talker . . . In intense noise and at low signal-to-noise ratios even unpracticed observers are able to improve their intelligibility test scores by as much as 30 percentage points by watching the talker's face.

The speech interference levels given by Peterson and Gross (1967:63) are equivalent to those given by Beranek (1954), though they are based on a new definition (Webster 1965). Since available noise spectra make the older definition more convenient, the following calculations use Beranek's figures.

The relation between speech interference level (SIL) and maximum distance, L, between speaker and listener may be very accurately represented by the empirical equation

$$\text{SIL (dB)} = 59.989 + v - 20.330 \log_{10} L(\text{ft.}), \qquad L > 0, \qquad (7.6)$$

where

$$v = 0(\text{normal voice}),$$
$$v = 6(\text{raised voice}), \text{ and}$$
$$v = 12(\text{very loud voice}).$$

This formula predicts the SILs of Table 7.4 with a maximum relative error of less than 0.006. For all practical purposes, $\text{SIL} = 60 - 20 \log_{10} L$ is sufficient. This approximation reproduces Webster's (1965:694) rule that "at any single criterion level, say 70 percent correct, for each doubling of the distance between talker and listener, 6 dB less noise can be tolerated." The upper range of validity of (7.6) is somewhere less than 1000 feet, at which distance the predicted SIL is less than zero and the attenuation due to air alone (25 to 60 percent relative humidity) at 1000 cycles per second (cps) is 17 dB (Beranek 1954:311). For the range of distances involved here, (7.6) is adequate.

Given a maximum distance L (the diameter of a circumscribing circle) between speaker and listener and a minimum distance d (minimum length of side) between any two people, the maximum number of people in a polygonal group is the largest integer k satisfying

$$\frac{d}{2} \le \frac{L}{2} \sin \frac{\pi}{k}. \qquad (7.7)$$

Thus,

$$k = \text{integer part of } \frac{\pi}{\sin^{-1}(d/L)} \quad \text{if } d \le L, \qquad (7.8)$$
$$= 1 \quad \text{if } d > L.$$

Solving (7.6) for L and substituting into (7.8) gives a formula for the maximum size of group as a function of SIL. Figure 7.1 is a graph of the resulting function for normal and raised voices and for minimum distances $d = 1.5$ and 2 feet. It may be in cultures other than that of the United States that values like $d = 1$ or $d = 3$ are more correct. To obtain the actual maximum group size from Figure 7.1, it is neces-

143

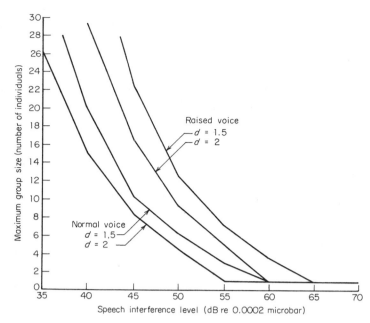

Figure 7.1 Predicted maximum size of group as a function of ambient speech interference level.

sary to take the integer part of the ordinate corresponding to any given SIL.

Now it is necessary to find the SILs corresponding to situations like those observed by James: pedestrians on sidewalks in downtown and residential areas; shopping groups; groups at play in playgrounds and nurseries; and public gatherings at picnics, a train depot, and beaches. The SIL can be calculated from the noise level spectrum of a situation by taking the arithmetic average of the sound pressure levels in the three bands 600–1200, 1200–2400, and 2400–4800 cps (Beranek 1954:419). (However, the average of the levels in the four octave bands between 300 and 4800 cps should be used instead if the levels in the 300–600 cps band are more than 10 dB above those in the 600–1200 cps band. This latter possibility never occurred with the spectra used below.)

Bonvallet (1950) observed the noise spectra of transportation vehicles at a distance of 20 feet. On the basis of his observations (1950:204, fig. 3), the average speech interference level of a 7-passenger sedan is 56 dB (flat net level re 0.0002 microbars), that of a trolley bus is 62 dB, and that of a subway car is 75 dB. The ranges in dB about the mean that include 50 percent of the vehicles observed are, respectively, 2.67 dB, 2.67 dB, and 3 dB. (These ranges are the averages of the ranges over the 400–3200 cps bands given in Bonvallet 1950:203, table 4.) Since sound levels are approximately normally distributed on the dB scale (see Bonvallet 1951:437, fig. 2), the speech interference level *above* which 99 percent of the observations fell may be calculated as mean $- 1.7 \times$ range. Thus, the SILs below which vehicle noise dropped only 1 percent of the time, at a distance of 20 feet, are 52 dB for an automobile, 58 dB for a trolley bus, and 70 dB for a subway car. These observations were made in Chicago under typical outdoor conditions in spring, summer, and fall. Reference to Figure 7.1 shows that pedestrians being passed by a stream of such automobiles could not form groups of more than 7 individuals if they spoke in a raised voice and maintained a distance of 2 feet from each other. If they spoke in a normal voice but permitted a distance of only 1.5 feet, the maximum group size would be 5. Since noise levels would be higher than these minima most of the time, most groups would have to be smaller. It is apparent from Figure 7.1 that not much increase would be required to drive the maximum group size to 1 or 2.

Bonvallet (1950) also reports the noise spectra inside vehicles in city traffic moving at typical speeds with all windows open. The calculated mean SILs that are below 99 percent of the cases, permitting the largest possible groups, are 53 dB for the automobile and 73 dB for the subway car. Figure 7.1 shows that the largest possible interacting group in an automobile is just in the vicinity of the maximum observed by Haight; even if automobiles had larger capacities, larger groups of people would not be able to hear each other over the noise. In a subway, speech communication is barely possible and only by shouting directly into a listener's ear; hence, one observes car after car full of isolates. Here is one predictable social consequence of technology.

Bonvallet confirms that the lower limit of noise levels

145

under heavy traffic conditions (1951:436, fig. 1), observed from a distance of 25–50 feet, leads to a speech interference level of 54 dB, limiting pedestrian group size to between 1 and 8, according to Figure 7.1 here, and most likely around 6. The lower extreme of noise in the daytime in residential areas in Chicago with traffic or industrial backgrounds leads to an SIL of 38 dB. Under these circumstances, larger groups than James observed are possible. (Still, as C. F. Mosteller observes, it is not very convenient to walk 6 abreast; there are other than acoustical constraints.)

Miller's (1960) sampling of New York traffic noise confirms that Bonvallet's results are not peculiar to Chicago. From an inner court of the seventeenth floor of the Biltmore Hotel, Miller measured the noise levels due to street traffic on a spring morning between 8:30 and 9:30 A.M. (1960:131, fig. 1). No nearby truck or bus noise was included. The minimum readings over this period of one hour on the slow meter gave an SIL of 54 dB (the maximum was 61 dB). Also in the spring, between 6:30 and 7:10 P.M., Miller measured the city traffic noise levels from outside an open window on the seventeenth floor of the Waldorf-Astoria Hotel, sampling in 15-second intervals on the slow meter. The minimum SIL calculated from his observations (1960:134, fig. 6) was 53 dB, and the maximum, 68 dB. These figures are very close to those reported by Bonvallet and lead to the same limitations on group size.

Finally, Cavanaugh et al. (1962: fig. 2) reported typical steady background noise levels in a general office area. The calculated SIL of 47 dB would prohibit groups of more than 7 if members were at least 2 feet distant from each other and spoke in a normal voice. But it is likely that in a general office area, and in private offices that have lower noise levels, requirements of work restrict group sizes more than does noise. In any event, James reports no observations of this situation.

Many of the above measurements and an excellent presentation of the problem of community noise generally are given by Stevens and Baruch (1957). Additional noise spectra taken from a variety of situations may be found in Beranek (1960: parts three and four); these seem generally to confirm the above results. For example, the SIL inside a 1959 automobile traveling with all windows closed at 70 miles per hour on a smooth asphaltic-concrete road is 55 dB for an upper-medium–priced make and 59 dB for a low-priced make (Beranek 1960:526). These values bracket Bonvallet's (1950) results on noise inside an automobile moving in city traffic with all windows open, which gave an average SIL of 57 dB.

If, as these results suggest, average and maximum casual group sizes are limited by average and minimum ambient SILs, then the average group sizes in two situations similar in all aspects but their SILs ought to vary inversely with those levels. Information from Haight and Coleman supports such a prediction. Coleman (1964:373) compared groups in Eugene, Oregon, a small city of 36,000 (in 1950, when James made his observations) with those in Portland, Oregon, a city of 374,000 (in 1950). Coleman noted without explanation that in each of three comparable situations (spring morning, spring afternoon, and department stores), the average group size was higher in Eugene than in Portland. It would seem that average street and traffic noises are probably higher in Portland than in Eugene.

On the basis of a single comparison, Coleman (1964:373) found a higher average group size in spring than in winter, out of doors. But indoors, on the basis of another single comparison, he found a higher average group size in winter than in spring. Bonvallet (1951:439) found that a blanket of snow covering the ground reduces traffic noises by 2 dB, and one would expect slightly larger groups outdoors during the winter. Here acoustical effects seem to be overridden by people's liking to be together outside in the spring and inside in the winter. Finally, Coleman (1964: 373) found his largest averages on public beaches and in school playgrounds. These open areas have the smallest amount of reflected noise due to surrounding buildings and are often more removed from traffic than downtown sidewalks. Also, children in these situations are willing to shout over noise. Thus, larger groups are reasonable.

While the pattern of relationships between noise levels and maximum group sizes displayed in this section is consistent with the belief that in some circumstances noise does limit group size, it must be emphasized that I have

147

done no direct, controlled experiments manipulating sound level and observing maximum or average group size. The argument is entirely inferential and may be affected by other, unknown factors.

The idea of linking the acoustics of speech communication and social behavior is not new. MacLean (1959) argued theoretically that cocktail parties could be classified as quiet or loud. When the (acoustically defined) well-mannered guests exceeded a certain critical number, which he calculated, the noise level of the party should make a sudden transition from quiet to loud. (See also the comments of Hardy 1959.) Though MacLean considered individuals to be distributed into conversational groups with one talker per group, he did not examine how those groups arise. In an empirical test of MacLean's theory, Legget and Northwood (1960) measured the sound pressure level (noise) at several scientific and professional receptions (including one for librarians) and found that the loudness increased fairly linearly from quiet to deafening as new guests arrived. The theoretical field remains open.

Sommer (1961) cited Schroeder (1962) as claiming that 8 feet is the upper limit of the arc of comfortable conversation. Sommer found from his own experiments that 5.5 feet nose-to-nose distance is the upper limit for a comfortable conversation, but he makes no mention of the ambient acoustical conditions. Since fairly comfortable conversations over much longer distances are commonly observed in classrooms and lectures, such an arbitrary limit is clearly not valid.

The above calculations do not explain why group sizes should approximate the truncated Poisson or truncated negative binomial distributions, but they do show why the parameters of those distributions must be nearly what they are. Thus, the social pattern is restricted, but not determined, by the conjunction of individual capacities to speak and to hear and the ecological levels of background noise. This linkage by explicit calculation of individual, social, and ecological measurements seems to be ardently desired by human ecologists (Kunkel 1967) but does not occur frequently in practice.

To extend this acoustical argument to the sleeping groups

of vervet monkeys would be perilous, since the groups were defined by criteria other than vocal communication and since nothing is known about the limits of intelligible communication among vervet monkeys. It is true that background noise in Amboseli Reserve, East Africa, is lower than in New York City, and therefore the people in East Africa should have larger or less crowded groups than they do in New York. As for the monkeys, the above argument should suggest only that there are individual and ecological factors that determine why the social parameters are what they are.

8
Critique
and
Conclusion

all ignorance toboggans into know
and trudges up to ignorance again:
    E. E. Cummings

O may the moon and sunlight seem
One inextricable beam,
For if I triumph I must make men mad.
    W. B. Yeats, *The Tower*

8.1 Critique

The matrix summarizing the matches between models or theoretical distributions and observed distributions or sets of data can now be completed. In Table 8.1 the substantial number of cases in which a model or distribution was not checked against applicable data (marked by "0") shows that my purpose was not to do unlikely models to death but, once satisfied of their improbability, to let them pass quietly.

In general, the LOST models account for the equilibrium and dynamics of data when we would expect them to and fail to describe equilibrial and dynamic data when we would expect them to fail. The winding path by which we reached this conclusion is summarized in Section 1.1.

It is not surprising that some theoretical dynamics or other turned out to be consistent with the theoretical equilibrium distribution of number of groups of each size; for, given $dn_i(t)/dt$ for all i and t, the equilibrium distribution follows by integration. However, there are many such dynamics $dn_i(t)/dt$, all consistent with the given equilibrium. What is surprising is that it was possible to guess a dynamics, simple in form, theoretically consistent with the known equilibrium, and empirically consistent with

Table 8.1. Matrix Summary of Matches Between Models or Theoretical
Distributions and Observed Distributions or Sets of Data

Data	Models or distributions								
	Truncated Poisson	Truncated negative binomial	Compound logarithmic	Truncated Poisson varying in time	Truncated Poisson varying over individuals	Combinatorial (Altmann)	Partitions	LOST Dynamics	Haight
James' "nice" data	+	0	x	x	x	x	0	x	0
Struhsaker's groups per night	x	x	−	x	x	−	+	x	x
Struhsaker's group sizes	−	+	x	−	−	0	+	x	±
Nursery school play	+	+	x	0	x	0	−	+	0
James' discrepant data	−	+	x	x	x	x	0	x	0
Lumsden monkey groups	+	0	0	x	x	x	−	x	−
Haight automobile occupancy	−	+	x	−	x	x	0	x	+
Richardson international alliances	−	−	x	x	x	x	0	x	0

Legend: + = good agreement
− = poor agreement
0 = model or distribution possibly applicable to data but agreement not checked
x = distribution not applicable to data or an analysis of model was not possible with detail available

151

new observations. Because of the substantial variability in the data, this success of the LOST models does not rule out the possibility of equal or greater success with the same and additional data on the part of more complicated, nonlinear models of dynamics. All that has been done is to approximate the linear, tangent plane of those more complicated models.

Having labored thus far, one may fairly ask whether the theoretical results and data presented here have any conceivable practical application. One possibility is to provide a firmer foundation for parts of epidemiology and the sociology of rumors.

The usual stochastic models of the spread of diseases or rumors through a mass of individuals (Bartlett 1960) ignore the formation of temporary associations among individuals in a population. If an individual who is diseased or misinformed joins a casual social group, then the likelihood of his spreading the disease or rumor to other members of his group is increased for the duration of his membership, while the likelihood for other members of the population of catching whatever he is spreading is decreased while he is in the group. Calculations of the time and frequency distributions of mutual exposure among members of populations behaving according to the LOST models, coupled with simple assumptions about the intragroup spread of disease or information, might yield more realistic models than those now available. (Lumsden 1951 was studying monkey sleeping groups to gain information about the epidemiology of sylvan yellow fever, but he presented no theoretical development to accompany his data.)

Before practical applications of the LOST models are undertaken with confidence, however, at least three remaining substantive problems with these models should receive better treatment: (1) the inadequacy of the quantity and quality of the data in support of the models; (2) the inadequacy of the theoretical approximations to the variance and covariance of the variables in the models; and (3) the inadequacy of the interpretation of the parameters in the models.

First, the claim that the distribution of the sizes of vervet monkey sleeping groups is well described by the truncated negative binomial distribution rests directly on Struhsaker's data, which are far superior in quality for these purposes to anything available before them. But his data are few; more such detailed data on these and other primates during their formation of groups for sleeping and for other social activities are needed. Additional data on freely forming or "spontaneous" groups (of human and nonhuman primates) should be used to check that the size distribution is indeed truncated negative binomial or truncated Poisson and that it is impossible to decompose the distribution into truncated Poisson components or to describe it by the combinatorial models.

The claim that the detailed social kinetics within a monkey troop may be described by the closed LOST model is an inference based not on direct evidence but on parsimony and unity of explanation. Observation of the detailed social kinetics of monkeys in appropriate situations should check this claim.

The data on the dynamics of human social groups presented here are also less than overwhelming in quantity and detail. In addition to checking whether the dynamics assumed actually occur among people other than four-year-olds, better data that identified the individuals belonging to each social group would make possible examination of the individual differences in social behavior. Such data may depend on fancier technology for making observations.

A second substantive problem is that the approximation to the variances and covariances of the numbers of groups of each size attempted in the Appendix to Chapter 4 should be replaced by an exact calculation. Such a calculation would provide a reliable foundation for tests of goodness of fit.

A third unsettled problem is the satisfactory interpretation of the parameters, especially b, of the LOST models. The parameter b specifies the proportionality of the rate of joining groups of size i to the number of individuals in those groups. When b is positive, the predicted distribution of group sizes is truncated negative binomial; when b is zero, the distribution is truncated Poisson. Why should b be positive in some situations (vervet sleeping groups, automobile occupancy, some days in the nursery school)

153

and zero in others (most of James's observations, Lumsden's monkey groups, perhaps other days in the nursery school)? A partial answer (Appendix B to Chapter 5) may be that in situations where the truncated Poisson distribution can fit the data, b is not truly zero but, rather, some small positive number hidden in the fluctuations of the data. Nursery school data set 2.142 (Valentine's Day, without the stories) may be an example of such a situation. The question then becomes: Why is b more positive in some situations than in others? A first guess might be that since b measures the attraction of individuals in groups, b might be expected to be higher in situations where individuals know each other than in situations where most people are strangers. Intuitively, in such situations one would expect relatively fewer isolates and more larger groups; this would in fact be predicted as b is increased. This suggestion is subject to experimental test by comparing rates of mixing and the equilibrium group size distributions of informal social situations in which the degree of prior acquaintance is varied.

The parameter c (Section 4.1) measures a tendency to depart that cannot be attributed either to independent individual behavior (measured by din_i) or to intragroup interactions (which would be measured by a term involving i^2). The implausibility of individual departures occurring at a rate that varies inversely according to group size thus seems consistent with the strictly mathematical argument (Section 4.2) that c must be zero.

Determining the meaning of the parameters in terms of the details of the social systems is a critical part of building confidence in the models' informativeness about reality. Without such checks, testing the model becomes more narrowly curve fitting; inferences to some real social process common to human and nonhuman primates, such as will be attempted in the concluding section, then become dangerous.

To emphasize this point, Table 8.2 presents some previously unpublished data kindly made available by P. A. Morris of the Royal Holloway College, University of London (personal communication, 20 May 1968). These data are the frequency distribution of the number of small mammals, or their remains, of various species found in

Table 8.2. Frequency Distribution of Small Mammals or Their Remains Trapped in Discarded Bottles in the British Isles

Size	Observed frequency	Truncated negative binomial
1	470	479.1
2	229	220.4
3	126	123.6
4	89	75.5
5	52	48.4
6	23	32.0
7	18	21.6
8	12	14.8
9	10	10.3
10	6	7.2
11	2	5.1
12	4	3.6
13	1	2.6
14	4	1.9
15	1	1.3
16	0	$1.7 \left\{ \begin{array}{l} 1.0 \\ 0.7 \end{array} \right.$
17	1	
$\geqslant 18^{a}$	3	1.9

$$p = 0.238$$
$$r = 0.208$$
$$x^2 = 13.427$$
$$df = 14$$
$$0.3 < P < 0.5$$

Data from P. A. Morris (personal communication 20 May 1968).
[a]The exact upper tail of the observations used in estimating parameters is one observation each with 18, 21, and 28 trapped animals.

1051 discarded bottles lying about the British countryside. A descriptive account and a frequency histogram based on a far smaller number of bottles were given by Morris and Harper (1965).

As Table 8.2 shows, the fit of this frequency distribution to the truncated negative binomial is excellent. It cannot be inferred, therefore, that the same social process that puts Californians into automobiles also traps shrews, voles, rats, and mice in discarded bottles. For one thing, the bottle that trapped the largest number of small mammals, a total

of 28, was a champagne bottle. More generally, all the sociological factors—perception of other groups and of individuals in other groups—assumed to be at work in the
LOST models appear absent here, and a variety of simple
probability models can account for the shape of this distribution. One possibility is that the distribution of numbers
of trapped mammals is a heterogeneous or mixed Poisson
(Section 2.1), with the heterogeneity provided by varying
sizes of bottle necks and capacities, varying population
densities of mammals in different regions, and varying
intervals of time between the discarding of the bottle and
the moment of observation. Another possibility derives the
negative binomial as a contagious distribution, the presence
of one mammal in a bottle increasing its attractiveness to
others (see Irwin 1941; Coleman 1964:326–332). Both possibilities are subject to experimental and observational
test; neither bears, nor should suggest, any similarity to
the sociological processes envisaged by the LOST models.

Let me conclude with two sets of data I have gathered
that have obdurately resisted satisfactory analysis by any
of the models or theoretical distributions so far presented.
Parts of one or the other set may be fitted by the truncated
negative binomial or by the Haight distribution; but neither
distribution can describe all of either set, according to the
criterion of the χ^2 test. (Each observation in these distributions, it will appear, is independent of the others, so
that test is appropriate.)

Table 8.3 presents the frequency distribution of sizes
of tourist parties visiting El Morro National Monument,
Highway 53, New Mexico. To gain access to the Inscription
Rock, which is the main attraction of the Monument, parties
must pass through the headquarters building where a National Park Service ranger asks a member of the party how
many people and how many automobiles are in his group.
Groups larger than 15 are lumped together in Table 8.3
since, according to the rangers, they were nearly always
arranged outings by business or scouting groups. (I am
grateful to the Monument's Supervisor, Mr. Paul A. Berger,
for access to the Park Service's daily records.)

The likelihood that tourist groups visiting a monument
in this remote area of New Mexico are more than casual

social groups is probably the source of the peaks in the frequency distributions for parties of sizes 2 and 4. The histograms were broken down by month to check and confirm the rangers' informal observations that both the absolute and the relative frequencies of group sizes altered from one season to another. The months in Table 8.3 are arranged not in chronological order but according to the cycle of the seasons.

Table 8.3. Frequency Distribution of Sizes of Tourist Parties Visiting El Morro National Monument, New Mexico, Six Selected Months in a Three-Year Period

Size of party	Dec. 1966	Jan. 1967	March 1968	May 1968	July 1967	Sept. 1967
1	29	11	18	39	55	47
2	65	52	86	227	261	212
3	15	12	29	75	123	93
4	21	18	37	79	172	66
5	10	5	20	50	123	36
6	12	8	16	26	77	20
7	7	1	4	13	46	7
8	2	1	2	9	29	10
9	1	0	5	8	13	8
10	0	0	2	1	3	0
11	1	1	1	3	1	3
12	0	0	0	2	4	4
13	0	0	0	2	2	0
14	0	0	1	0	1	0
15	0	0	0	0	2	2
>15	0	1	17	22	19	4

Data are compiled from National Park Service records, courtesy of Mr. Paul A. Berger. Parties larger than 15 are "organized outings."

An interesting secular trend in the parameters of this system is suggested by Table 8.4, which shows the number of visitors and cars during the peak summer months from 1962 to 1966. While the number of visitors rose steadily, the number of cars rose even faster, so that the mean number of passengers per car dropped steadily. It is not obvious to me how the kinds of models presented here would explain such secular trends.

Table 8.5 presents the frequency distribution of size of

Casual Groups of Monkeys and Men

Table 8.4. Total Number of Visitors and Cars at El Morro National Monument, New Mexico in May, June, July, and August 1962-1966

Year	Visitors	Cars	Average visitors per car
1962	9134	2096	4.36
1963	9381	2206	4.25
1964	10344	2439	4.24
1965	11998	2837	4.23
1966	12115	2973	4.08

Data from National Park Service, courtesy of Paul A. Berger.

parties making reservations for dinner (after 5 P.M.) at Novak's, a fancy restaurant in Brookline, Massachusetts, during the first 98 days of 1968. (I thank Mr. Robert Novak for access to Novak's reservation book.) Frequency distributions are given for each day of the week, since that seemed to affect the absolute and relative frequencies. To give some idea of the variability within each day of the week, each day's observations are further decomposed into those during the first seven weeks of the year and those during the second seven weeks of the year.

Since there was a good financial incentive to keep the reservation book accurate, probably all reservations requested are recorded there. But Mr. Novak pointed out that the likelihood that a party will make a reservation before coming to the restaurant increases sharply with the party's size. Hence, any model that attempts to account for these data must not only generate an underlying distribution of party size but must also propose a probability mechanism for how those parties are recorded.

Like the data from El Morro, these distributions peak at parties of even size, suggesting that the fundamental unit of aggregation here may be the couple rather than the individual. The truncated negative binomial distribution could not be expected to describe these data, nor does it. Unfortunately, at least with the present means of estimating parameters, neither does the Haight distribution, in general. These data offer an open invitation to modeling.

158

Table 8.5. Frequency Distribution of Size of Parties Reserving Dinner at Novak's, Brookline, Massachusetts, During the First 98 Days of 1968[a]

Size of party	Monday I	Monday II	Tuesday I	Tuesday II	Wednesday I	Wednesday II	Thursday I	Thursday II	Friday I	Friday II	Saturday I	Saturday II	Sunday I	Sunday II
1	1	0	0	0	0	0	0	0	1	1	1	1	0	2
2	30	9	25	36	80	77	37	51	113	136	138	166	62	83
3	10	9	14	26	30	37	18	33	62	56	24	24	38	40
4	18	14	17	29	43	44	27	46	83	84	152	171	61	111
5	11	5	7	7	18	19	7	14	15	25	19	19	26	19
6	3	5	4	5	12	10	5	11	22	12	44	46	23	24
7	4	4	1	4	4	4	3	9	5	8	5	9	9	7
8	2	5	2	1	5	1	1	2	2	6	28	11	10	4
9	0	0	0	0	2	3	1	2	0	5	1	4	0	3
10	2	1	2	0	1	1	3	3	0	7	8	3	2	2
11	0	0	0	2	2	0	0	0	0	0	1	2	2	2
12	0	0	1	0	1	3	2	1	0	0	1	3	2	2
13	1	0	0	0	0	0	0	0	0	1	0	1	2	3
14	0	0	0	1	0	0	0	0	0	0	0	0	0	0
15	1	1	0	0	0	0	1	0	0	1	1	0	0	2
>15	1	0	0	1	0	0	1	1	1	0	0	0	2	0

Data compiled from Novak's reservation book, courtesy of Robert Novak.

[a] "I" gives frequency on each day during first 7 weeks; "II" gives frequency during second 7 weeks.

To criticize a work for what it did not attempt is a privilege usually reserved to reviewers for the public press. Yet I must point out what these last two examples imply (and what is obvious): there is more to the social phenomena of cooperation and hostility, leadership, organization, and disintegration than the present models can account for. Slater's finding (1958) that the optimal size of task-oriented groups by some criterion was around 5 contrasts with the finding here that most casual (not task-oriented) groups are of size 1 and 2. The whole tradition of research represented by Hare, Borgatta, and Bales (1965) offers a quite different perspective on small groups. Problems in the social psychology of industry do not melt into solution in the face of the kinds of models presented here. Explanations of all the enormous diversity of animal social

159

organization (Wynne-Edwards 1962: esp. chaps. 1 and 8) do not suddenly appear. That the models of this book do not answer all questions does not contradict that they answer a few, but affirms that there are still good questions to ask.

8.2 Conclusion

Between the behavior of individuals and the evolution of populations stands the social organization of a species. In *The Republic,* Plato modeled the state simply by scaling up the functions and parts of the individual, a mode of thought frequently adopted since. Freud (1915–1916) wrote of "the obvious analogy between deformities of character resulting from protracted sickliness in childhood and the behavior of whole nations whose past history has been full of suffering."

The work of Allee (1938) and his colleagues in the field of mass physiology showed that direct changes of scale from organism to aggregation are invalid all over the phylogenetic tree. Practically any animal is affected, for better or worse, by the presence of other animals of his species. Wilson (1967) has emphasized the inutility and confusing effect of thinking of colonies of the social insects as large organisms. And Horvath and Foster (1963) showed in at least one case that the social kinetics of nations is not the social kinetics of men.

Primatologists often prefer to extrapolate from the family, to ask whether groups are not based simply on familial and mating relations. Struhsaker (1965) attempted to explain all the pairings he found in sleeping groups using known and probable familial relations, but he did not claim to succeed. Clearly, such an attempt would also fail for many of the human groups observed by James, though it might explain many of them. Such failures are not biologically surprising. Allee (1938:48) cites several animal social aggregations that are not based on family ties.

Schools of fish arise, for example, under conditions in which there is no association with either parent after the eggs are laid. At times the eggs may be so scattered in the laying that the schools form from unrelated individuals. Here the schooling tendency seems to underlie rather than grow out of family life.

Though familial ties are a potent partial explanation of groupings observed among monkeys and men they are not a sufficient explanation.

It may be more productive theoretically to seek other grounds for explanation that include the scope of familial ties. The stochastic models of this study are proposed as an example of a more general and inclusive explanation. Familial ties could be represented within the LOST models by assuming higher rates of attraction (arrival) and lower rates of repulsion (departure) for related groups and individuals and lower attraction and higher repulsion for unrelated groups and individuals. If this embedding of familial ties within the model were successful, then the average arrival and departure rates would equal those estimated from the equilibrial distribution of group sizes.

Supposing that the LOST models, or some family of models like them, are acceptable characterizations of the formation of casual or spontaneous groups among vervets, humans, and possibly other primates, what kinds of evolutionary inferences can be drawn? The naive comparative strategy ("Go to the ant, thou sluggard; consider her ways, and be wise") is as antique as Plato's and as often abused. It is not sufficient to illuminate the phylogeny of societies.

Simpson (1958:10–12) has presented three grounds for evolutionary or historical inference in studies, like this one, that have as data organisms, their activities, and the conditions surrounding and influencing them but that lack any sequences of observations over geological time.

(1) Related lineages often evolve more or less in parallel but some faster than others; at any one time, then, the contemporaneous representatives of the various lineages may form a series that approximates the historical sequence leading to the more advanced members of the group. (2) Certain historical trends (e.g., from smaller to larger size, from simpler to more complex behavior) are

161

so frequent or logical that they may be assumed to have occurred in a given case. (3) Characteristics shared by contemporaneous organisms are likely to have been present in their common ancestry.

If several primate species are found to have social groupings described by variants of the LOST models, then the third of Simpson's rules of inference leads to the conclusion that in the ancestral primate stock, individuals formed casual groups through the kinds of attractions and repulsions specified by the LOST models. This conclusion must be qualified by pointing out a pitfall associated with the third rule of inference, that "parallelism and convergence in evolution have been extremely common and they produce resemblances not present in a common ancestor" (Simpson 1958:12). To guard against this pitfall, primates from a substantial variety of environments should be compared.

Recall that in many of the human cases observed so far, the truncated Poisson distribution sufficed; the rate of attraction due to individuals, specified by parameter b, was zero or some small positive value. In the case of the vervets, that parameter b was substantially positive. If it should develop that, as the species of primate observed advances from prosimian to man, the average value of b for each species decreases toward zero (this is sheer speculation now), then by Simpson's first rule of inference there may be some evolutionary reason for the attraction of a group due to the individuals in it to diminish in geological time relative to the attraction of simple group membership. This first rule of inference also has its pitfalls:

a contemporaneous series may not at all resemble an ancestral sequence; different characteristics commonly evolve at different rates so that the animal most primitive in one respect may be most advanced in another . . . (Simpson 1958:12).

I see no way of checking this possibility, except through the discovery of a statistically useful number of fossilized social groups—a remote possibility.

Were a sequence of historically decreasing values of b

plausibly established, the remaining evolutionary problem would be to explain why. I refrain here from commit-
ting a speculation upon a speculation.

The LOST models deal with only one narrow aspect of
social life, namely, size of group. Thompson (1958) identi-
fies other aspects: cohesiveness (amount of scatter); syn-
tality (amount of action in concert); stability (fixedness of
interindividual relations); and permeability (openness to
strange individuals). After pointing out the interest of these
characteristics of social life, Thompson (1958:308) arrived
at a "perhaps disappointing . . . broad generalization . . . In
summary, it may be stated that the evolution of social behavior is a broad and complex problem."

If explicit models like the LOST models were available
for all the aspects of social life identified by Thompson and
if historical sequences of their parameter values could be
estimated or inferred, then, and only then (I believe), it
would be possible to attach full meaning to the phrase "the
phylogenetic evolution of societies." The evolution would
consist in the trajectory of the parameters of the models,
and a theory of the evolution of social behavior would consist in a theory of that trajectory.

According to this definition of the phylogeny of societies,
this study is only a precise description in unifying language
of some of the comparative building blocks of an evolutionary theory. It is a long way from being that theory.

Near the end of his wonderfully suggestive book, *Childhood and Society,* the psychoanalyst Erikson (1963:419)
cautions:

. . . in the use of reason lies the eternal temptation to do
with human data in experiment and argument what the
child does with them in play: namely, to reduce them to
a size and an order in which they seem manageable.
Thus human data are treated as if the human being were
an animal, or a machine, or a statistical item. Much naive
sense of power can be derived from the fact that,
properly approached, the human being up to a point is
all of these things, and under certain conditions can be
reduced to being nothing but their facsimiles. But the
attempt to make man more exploitable by reducing him
to a simpler model of himself cannot lead to an
essentially human psychology.

163

The approach to man taken here is not a denial that there is more to man than an animal, a machine, or a digit. A more individualistic psychology will be required to explain even the differences discovered among the vervets. The guiding idea in this work is that much of what may seem proper to an essentially human psychology, sociology, and ecology may actually be part of a more general evolutionary psychology, sociology, and ecology, and that it is not a denigration, but a comfort, to see the laws and freedoms of men as some of the laws and freedoms of life.

Allee, W. C. *The Social Life of Animals.* New York: Norton, 1938.

Altmann, Stuart A. "Mathematical Models of Random Subgroup Formation" (Abstract), *American Zoologist,* vol. 5, no. 4 (November 1965), 420.

―――― *Social Communication Among Primates.* Chicago: University of Chicago Press, 1967.

Anscombe, F. J. "Sampling Theory of the Negative Binomial and Logarithmic Series Distributions," *Biometrika,* vol. 37 (1950), 358–382.

Bartlett, M. S. *Stochastic Population Models in Ecology and Epidemiology.* New York: Wiley, 1960.

Barton, D. E., F. N. David, and M. Merrington. "Tables for the Solution of the Exponential Equation, $\exp(-a) + ka = 1$," *Biometrika,* vol. 47 (1960), 439–445.

Batchelder, Paul M. *An Introduction to Linear Difference Equations.* Cambridge, Mass.: Harvard University Press, 1927.

Beranek, Leo L. *Acoustics.* New York: McGraw-Hill, 1954.

―――― *Noise Reduction.* New York: McGraw-Hill, 1960.

Bliss, C. I., and R. A. Fisher. "Fitting the Negative Binomial Distribution to Biological Data" and "Note on the Efficient Fitting of the Negative Binomial," *Biometrics,* vol. 9 (June 1953), 176–200.

Bonvallet, G. L. "Levels and Spectra of Transportation Vehicle Noise," *Journal of the Acoustical Society of America,* vol. 22, no. 2 (March 1950), 201–205.

―――― "Levels and Spectra of Traffic, Industrial, and Residential Area Noise," *Journal of the Acoustical Society of America,* vol. 23, no. 4 (July 1951), 435–439.

Brass, W. "Simplified Methods of Fitting the Truncated Negative Binomial Distribution," *Biometrika,* vol. 45 (1958), 59–68.

Cavanaugh, W. J., et al. "Speech Privacy in Buildings," *Journal of the Acoustical Society of America,* vol. 34, no. 4 (April 1962), 475–492.

Cochran, W. G. "Some Methods for Strengthening the Common χ^2 Test," *Biometrics,* vol. 10 (1954), 417–451.

Cohen, A. Clifford, Jr. "Estimating the Parameter in a Conditional Poisson Distribution," *Biometrics,* vol. 16 (1960), 203–211.

165

Coleman, James S. *Introduction to Mathematical Sociology.* New York: Free Press, 1964.

Coleman, James S., and John James. "The Equilibrium Size Distribution of Freely Forming Groups," *Sociometry*, vol. 24 (1961), 36–45.

David, F. N., and N. L. Johnson. "The Truncated Poisson," *Biometrics*, vol. 8 (1952), 275–285.

DeVore, Irven, ed. *Primate Behavior: Field Studies of Monkeys and Apes.* New York: Holt, Rinehart and Winston, 1965.

Erikson, Erik H. *Childhood and Society.* New York: Norton, 1963.

Etkin, William. "Cooperation and Competition in Social Behavior," in *Social Behavior and Organization Among Vertebrates*, W. Etkin, ed. Chicago: University of Chicago Press, 1964, pp. 1–34.

Feller, William. *An Introduction to Probability Theory and Its Applications*, Vol. 1, 2nd ed. New York: Wiley, 1957.

Fisher, R. A. *Statistical Methods for Research Workers*, 13th ed. New York: Hafner, 1958.

Foster, F. G. "A Markov Chain Derivation of Discrete Distributions," *Annals of Mathematical Statistics*, vol. 23 (1952), 624–627.

Freud, Sigmund. "Some Character-Types Met With in Psychoanalytic Work," *Imago* 4, 1915–1916. Reprinted in translation in *Character and Culture*, Philip Rieff, ed. New York: Collier, 1962, pp. 157–181.

Goodman, Leo A. "Mathematical Methods for the Study of Systems of Groups," *American Journal of Sociology*, vol. 70 (1964), 170–192.

Gupta, Hansraj, C. E. Gwyther, and J. C. P. Miller. *Tables of Partitions*, Royal Society Mathematical Tables, vol. 4. Cambridge: University Press, 1958.

Haight, F. A. *A Statistical Examination of Vehicle Occupancy in Los Angeles*, Research Report No. 31, Institute of Transportation and Traffic Engineering, University of California, Los Angeles, May 1960.

——— *Handbook of the Poisson Distribution.* New York: Wiley, 1967.

Hamilton, W. D. "The Genetical Evolution of Social Behavior," *Journal of Theoretical Biology*, vol. 7 (1964), 1–52.

Hardy, Howard C. "Cocktail Party Acoustics," *Journal of the Acoustical Society of America*, vol. 31, no. 4 (April 1959), 535.

Hare, A. Paul, Edgar F. Borgatta, and Robert F. Bales, *Small Groups: Studies in Social Interaction*, rev. ed. New York: Knopf, 1965.

Hawley, Mones E., and Karl D. Kryter, "Effects of Noise on Speech," in *Handbook of Noise Control,* Cyril M. Harris, ed. New York: McGraw-Hill, 1957, chap. 9.

Henshel, Richard L. "Some Convergences between Maslow's Primate Dominance Studies and a Theory of Human Coalitions by T. Caplow; A Proposal for Further Investigation," *Primates,* vol. 4, no. 4 (1963), 79–83.

Hildebrand, F. B. *Introduction to Numerical Analysis.* New York: McGraw-Hill, 1956.

Hirata, Shinzo. "The Movement of People at the Ticket Office of Shinzyuku Station" (in Japanese), *Kagaku (Science),* vol. 3 (1933), 274–275.

Horvath, William J., and Caxton C. Foster. "Stochastic Models of War Alliances," *Journal of Conflict Resolution,* vol. 7, no. 2 (1963), 110–116.

Irwin, J. O. "Comments on the Paper 'Chambers, E. C. and Yule, G. U., Theory and Observation in the Investigation of Accident Causation,'" *Journal of the Royal Statistical Society* (Supplement), vol. 7 (1941), 89–109.

James, John, "A Preliminary Study of the Size Determinant in Small Group Interaction," *American Sociological Review,* vol. 16 (1951), 474–477.

—— "The Distribution of Free-Forming Small Group Size," *American Sociological Review,* vol. 18 (1953), 569–570.

Katz, Leo. "Characteristics of Frequency Functions Defined by First Order Difference Equations," Ph.D. dissertation, University of Michigan, Ann Arbor, 1945.

—— "On the Class of Functions Defined by the Difference Equation $(x + 1)f(x + 1) = (a + bx)f(x)$" (Abstract), *Annals of Mathematical Statistics,* vol. 17 (1946), 501.

—— "The Distribution of the Number of Isolates in a Social Group," *Annals of Mathematical Statistics,* vol. 23 (1952), 271–276.

—— "United Treatment of a Broad Class of Discrete Probability Distributions," in *Classical and Contagious Discrete Distributions,* G. P. Patil, ed. New York: Pergamon, 1965, pp. 175–182.

Kendall, David G. "Stochastic Processes and Population Growth," *Journal of the Royal Statistical Society,* Series B, vol. 11, no. 2 (1949), 230–264.

Kendall, Maurice G. and Alan Stuart. *The Advanced Theory of Statistics,* Vol. 1. London: Griffin, 1958.

Kunkel, John H. "Some Behavioral Aspects of the Ecological Approach to Social Organization," *American Journal of Sociology,* vol. 73, no. 1 (1967), 12–29.

Legget, R. F. and T. D. Northwood, "Noise Surveys of Cocktail

Parties," *Journal of the Acoustical Society of America*, vol. 32, no. 1 (January 1960), 16–18.

Lehmer, Derrick H. "The Machine Tools of Combinatorics," in *Applied Combinatorial Mathematics*, Edwin F. Beckenbach, ed. New York: Wiley, 1964, pp. 5–31.

Lumsden, W. H. R. "The Night-Resting Habits of Monkeys in a Small Area on the Edge of the Semliki Forest, Uganda: A Study in Relation to the Epidemiology of Sylvan Yellow Fever," *Journal of Animal Ecology*, vol. 20 (1951), 11–30.

MacLean, William R. "On the Acoustics of Cocktail Parties," *Journal of the Acoustical Society of America*, vol. 31, no. 1 (January 1959), 79–80.

Miller, Laymon N. "A Sampling of New York City Traffic Noise," *Noise Control*, vol. 6, no. 3 (May–June 1960), 131–135.

Morris, P. A. and J. F. Harper. "The Occurrence of Small Mammals in Discarded Bottles," *Proceedings of the Zoological Society of London*, vol. 145, no. 1 (June 1965), 148–153.

Mosteller, C. Frederick and John W. Tukey. "Data Analysis, Including Statistics," in *Revised Handbook of Social Psychology*, G. Lindzey and E. Aronson, eds. Reading, Mass.: Addison-Wesley, 1968.

Patil, Ganapati P., and Sharadchandra W. Joshi. *A Dictionary and Bibliography of Discrete Distributions*. Edinburgh and London: Oliver and Boyd, 1968.

Peterson, Arnold P. G., and Ervin E. Gross, Jr. *Handbook of Noise Measurement*, 6th ed. West Concord, Mass.: General Radio Company, 1967.

Quenouille, M. H. "A Relation Between the Logarithmic, Poisson and Negative Binomial Series," *Biometrics*, vol. 5, no. 2 (1949), 162–164.

Rao, C. R. and I. M. Chakravarti. "Some Small Sample Tests of Significance for a Poisson Distribution," *Biometrics*, vol. 12 (1956), 264–282.

Rider, Paul R. "Truncated Binomial and Negative Binomial Distributions," *Journal of the American Statistical Association*, vol. 50 (1955), 877–883.

Sampford, M. R. "The Truncated Negative Binomial Distribution," *Biometrika*, vol. 42 (1955), 58–69.

Schroeder, Francis de Neufville. *Anatomy for Interior Designers*, 3rd ed., Julius Panero, ed. New York: Whitney Library of Design (Hill and Wang), 1962.

Shenton, L. R., and R. Myers. "Comments on Estimation for the Negative Binomial Distribution," in *Classical and Contagious Discrete Distributions*, G. P. Patil, ed. New York: Pergamon, 1965, 241–262.

Simpson, George Gaylord. "The Study of Evolution: Methods and Present Status of Theory," in *Behavior and Evolution,* Anne Roe and G. G. Simpson, eds. New Haven: Yale University Press, 1958, 7–26.

Slater, Philip. "Contrasting Correlates of Group Size," *Sociometry,* vol. 21, no. 1 (March 1958), 129–139.

Sommer, Robert, "Leadership and Group Geography," *Sociometry,* vol. 24, no. 1 (March 1961), 99–110.

Stevens, K. N., and J. J. Baruch. "Community Noise and City Planning," in *Handbook of Noise Control,* Cyril M. Harris, ed. New York: McGraw-Hill, 1957, chap. 35.

Struhsaker, Thomas T. "Behavior of the Vervet Monkey *(Cercopithecus aethiops),*" Ph.D. dissertation, University of California, Berkeley, 1965.

———— "Behavior of Vervet Monkeys and Other Cercopithecines," *Science,* vol. 156 (1967a), 1197–1203.

———— *Behavior of Vervet Monkeys* (Cercopithecus aethiops), University of California Publications in Zoology, Vol. 82, Berkeley and Los Angeles: University of California Press, 1967b.

———— "Social Structure Among Ververt Monkeys *(Cercopithecus aethiops),*" *Behavior,* vol. 29 (1967c), 83–121.

———— "Auditory Communication Among Vervet Monkeys *(Cercopithecus aethiops),*" in *Social Communication Among Primates,* Stuart A. Altmann, ed. Chicago: University of Chicago Press, 1967d, 281–324.

Sukhatme, P. V. "On the Distribution of χ^2 in Samples of the Poisson Series," *Journal of the Royal Statistical Society* (Supplement), vol. 5 (1938), 75–79.

Terao, Senzo. "On the Distribution of Combined Pedestrians" (in Japanese), *Oyobuturi (Journal of Applied Physics),* vol. 18, no. 4 (1949).

Thompson, William R. "Social Behavior," in *Behavior and Evolution,* Anne Roe and G. G. Simpson, eds. New Haven: Yale University Press, 1958, 291–310.

Webster, J. C. "Speech Communications as Limited by Ambient Noise," *Journal of the Acoustical Society of America,* vol. 37, no. 4 (April 1965), 692–699.

West, Mary Jane. "Foundress Associations in Polistine Wasps: Dominance Hierarchies and the Evolution of Social Behavior," *Science,* vol. 157 (September 1967), 1584–1585.

White, Harrison C. "Chance Models of Systems of Casual Groups," *Sociometry,* vol. 25 (1962), 153–172.

Wilson, Edward O. "The Superorganism Concept and Beyond," in *L'Effet de Groupe Chez les Animaux,* Centre National de la Recherche Scientifique, Paris: 1967.

**Casual Groups
of
Monkeys
and Men**

Wynne-Edwards, V. C. *Animal Dispersion in Relation to Social Behaviour,* Edinburgh and London: Oliver and Boyd, 1962.

Index

Acoustical theory, 7, 148–149. *See also* Noise levels

Aiken Computation Laboratory, 57

Allee, W. C., 160

Alliances for war, international, 7, 54, 131–132, 160

Altmann, Stuart A., 10; and group formation, 35–37; combinatorial model of, 42–43; and dominance, 138

Amboseli Reserve, East Africa, 149

Anderson, Donald G. M., 57

Anscombe, F. J., 23

Bales, Robert F., 159

Bartlett, M. S., 45, 152; and equilibrium variance, 65, 66

Barton, D. E., 19

Baruch, J. J., and community noise, 146

Batchelder, Paul M., hypergeometric equation by, 68, 69–70

Beranek, Leo L.: and speech interference levels, 141–142, 143, 144; his observations of noise spectra, 146, 147

Berger, Paul A., 156

Biltmore Hotel, observations of traffic noise at, 146

Binomial distribution: and LOST model, 52; of isolation, 133–134

Bliss, C. I., on negative binomial distribution, 23, 30

Bonvallet, G. L., on noise, 144–146, 147

Borgatta, Edgar F., 159

Bottled mammals, 154–156

Brass, W.: method for fitting truncated negative binomial distribution, 30–34, 118, 131; and jackknife, 92, 94, 100, 101, 103, 109–110

Cambridge Nursery School, observations at, 5–6, 72–74, 110, 123

Cavanaugh, W. J., on noise levels, 146

Cercopithecine monkeys, 11. *See also* Vervet monkeys

Cercopithecus aethiops, see Vervet monkeys

Chakravarti, I. M., 21

χ^2 test, 16, 19, 31, 82, 106, 156; compared with X^2, 20n; applied to monkey sleeping groups, 23, 120–121; rejections by, 126–128

Closed systems, 44–50; defined, 5, 9; approach of, to equilibrium, 55–65

Cochran, W. G., and χ^2 test, 20, 20n, 135

Cocktail parties, noise levels at, 148

Cohen, A. Clifford, Jr., and Poisson distribution, 19, 21, 26, 32

Coleman, James S., 52, 156; and freely forming groups, 8–10, 141; and Poisson distribution, 24, 25, 49–50; on "sociological" models, 44; and frequency distributions of group size, 118, 126; and Yule distribution, 131; on group size and noise level, 147

Colobus abyssinicus ituricus, 122

Comfortable conversation, 148

Contagious models, 49–50, 156

Cummings, E. E., 150

David, F. N., 19

Detention time (DT), 96–99; defined, 96–97